BE A LION

TERRY BLACKBURN

POWERHOUSE
PUBLICATIONS

COPYRIGHT

DISCLAIMER

The author has taken liberties with the geographical location of the animals in this book. He's aware that lions and sloths come from different parts of the world.

Can any poachers therefore please hold their fire.

DEDICATION

This book is dedicated to my amazing children Ellie and Theo, my unborn child due this summer, my step-son Jude, my amazing partner Louise, and my mum Janice.

I would also like to thank 3 key people who influenced my success over the years: Jason Howard, Tony Taylor and Richard Coulson. I am so glad I met you all and so grateful for your guidance, advice, and support.

And a big shout to Lee Flanagan, my best friend and colleague in business for many years, as well as everyone who has helped me on my journey of success this far.

Without all of you, and many more, I would not be in the position I am in my life.

I am forever grateful for you all.

CONNECT WITH ME

Take pictures of your journey as a lion – include photos of yourself; sections of this book that you find helpful; quotes that you like; your list of goals, etc. Then, post it and tag me on Instagram.

Contents

THE WILDERNESS

CONNECT WITH ME

Take pictures of your journey as a lion – include photos of yourself; sections of this book that you find helpful; quotes that you like; your list of goals, etc. Then, post it and tag me on Instagram.

KINGS OF THE JUNGLE

Lions are the kings of the jungle. They are the dominant animals in many locations and habitats – they live the life they want on their own terms. They don't have any self-doubt, any worries or issues. They just dominate their lives and do whatever they want whenever they want.

You too can live a life where you do what you want when you want with zero self-doubt.

Lions don't see a gazelle or a zebra walking past and think, *I'm not good enough to eat today or go and catch that zebra. No*, they go and run after that zebra with no self-doubt at all. They get shit done and get what they want on their terms.

This is the kind of life you can have with the correct mindset. Throughout this book, I will explain how lion mentality applies to business, property, health, fitness and relationships.

Many of the most successful people across the world in all walks of life have this lion mentality. Read on to find out exactly how to live this way.

There are many similarities with other animals and how they live their lives that you may be able to relate to – we will also cover these in this book. For example, hyenas. Now, these creatures are always laughing or making fun of other people. They are sly and manipulative, they aren't trustworthy and they're not the kind of people you want around you.

I'm sure you can think of people who are like this – whether they were at school, at work, your friend's family or even a partner. Avoid these mood hoovers at all costs.

What does a lion do if a hyena is annoying him? Probably bite his head off or something along those lines. Now, for the record, please don't go and bite off another human's head. That would be bad!

However, be aware that a lion mentality is needed when dealing with these types of people: avoid them, walk away, block them, do whatever is needed to avoid them in your life. if there are one or two in your life, it's easy to get rid of them.

However, even the strongest lions can be overpowered by a pack of hyenas. If you have a pack of them around you, it's only a matter of time before they drag you down with them or down to their shallow level in the dirt of the jungle or wilderness.

Now, in life, there are also other people who have similarities to sloths. Sloths are slow creatures who do very little in their lives, slowly move around the trees, slowly eating leaves and everything else they eat. Now, I'm sure we all know some people who do very little in life – going through the motions and just "getting by". Don't be one of these type of people. They do not know what life is about and never really amount to anything.

I hope you have a desire to read on now, as the analogies get more detailed and more relevant and you can apply the lion mindset to every part of your life. This book will raise your own awareness of when and where you should act like a lion, how to identify the hyenas and sloths in your life, now and in the future. In addition, how to stay well away from them and minimise contact with them for a more fulfilled happy, healthy and wealthy life and live the life of your wildest dreams. Because guess what?

It is possible …

One lion can't take down an elephant by itself. But 10 strong lions working together can.

HOW TO TAKE DOWN AN ELEPHANT

Knowing what I know now, I've got everything I could dream of. I'm really healthy and spend an hour in the gym most mornings. I've got an amazing partner and kids. I've got incredible friends. I've set up seven businesses: one of them is the most successful life insurance and mortgage brokers in the country. I own a portfolio of properties and I've just won a prestigious award for property investing in the UK. I also present my own podcast with some of the most successful millionaires and billionaires appearing as guests on the show. I'm 32 and I feel like I've only just got started with what I'm intending to achieve in my lifetime …

Back when I was a kid, things were very different. I had big dreams but no idea of how to go about achieving them. My teachers used to put me down and tell me I'd never amount to anything. After I left school, I ended up in a job I hated as a builder, with people in charge of me who laughed at me and told me to forget my dreams.

I know these people now as 'poachers' – people who stalk lions and take pleasure in killing their dreams. Yes, I had dreams back then, but there were times when I wondered if I would ever achieve them at all. I certainly never would have thought it was possible to achieve what I have today. But I'm jumping ahead of myself ...

This is a book for you if you're unhappy with the life you're currently living. It's for you if you feel like a hamster trapped on a wheel spinning round and round in a job you don't enjoy. It's for you if you're fed up with being ordered around by your boss and want to set up your own business. It's for you if you want to learn about passive income so you can leave a legacy for you children and your grandchildren. It's for you if there's a fire burning in you for something bigger than the life you're currently experiencing and you're looking for clues for what you need to do to make a massive success of your life.

I'm often asked how I've been so successful, how I manage my time, why I'm constantly setting new goals for myself and how I achieve them. In this book, I'm going to share my journey with you and the tips and strategies that helped me achieve my dreams. My message to you is that you can do this too. You just have to believe it. Then, you have to take action.

But first, let me ask you: could one lion take down a huge elephant by itself? Probably not, even though it might have a go. But could 10 strong lions working together take down the same elephant? More than likely! You need the help of others to achieve big things. You also need the help of books, content and coaches to achieve big things – hence why this book is so important to your future success.

Lions have a lot of teach us when it comes to success and having the right kind of mindset. It's these principles I'd like to share with you in my book. I've always found that people tend to remember ideas much better when they have an analogy or a visual picture in their mind. So the lion is a powerful symbol that you can use to help you achieve success.

When people think of a lion, they think of confidence, nobility, courage, strength and power. They tend to think of the 'Lord of the Jungle.'

A lion symbolises confidence, nobility, courage, strength and power.

What they tend to forget is that most lions live in prides of up to 40 – and they are stronger working as a pride than when they are alone. Yes, they can be loners, wandering across the savannah on their own. But they can take down bigger prey and have a bigger territory when they work together as a pride.

So there are many similarities between lions and people who win in life in general. Lions don't limit themselves as to what they can achieve. If they want something – a gazelle, a zebra, a wildebeest – they just go after it. If they don't succeed, if it outruns them, or escapes, they don't feel sorry for themselves or give up. They dust themselves off and try again. They have ZERO self-doubt.

A lion has always been a very important symbol for me – both in my personal life and my business life. It symbolises strength, power, focus, winning, being unstoppable and getting things done.

When a rival lion comes into your life and tries to take what you have – as often happens in both business and life – you need to have a pride that has your back, so you are strong enough mentally, physically, financially, to fight back and win.

Lions do a lot of things together. They communicate well with one another and enjoy relaxing as much as hunting. When they hunt, each one has a specific role it plays. Some will play the role of 'centres' and others are 'wings' that push the prey towards the centre. The more lions are involved in the hunt, the more successful they are. In majority of successes in business, property, life, health or fitness, the bigger and more skilled and experienced your team is, the bigger the things you can achieve. The bigger your sales team in business the more sales you will make. The bigger your power team in property (from solicitors to builders, contacts with estate agents and your network) the more property you will generally find. The more people you have to help you get fitter (personal trainers, nutritionists, mindset coaches, support from partner/friends/family) the more likely you are to get fit.

They all roar together to warn other animals away and even the cubs join in. As a result, the roaring can be heard 5 miles away. That's teamwork for you!

When you think like a lion, you get things done – especially if you mix with other lions who are similar to you.

However, if you're a lion, there are certain animals you should try to avoid. Hyenas, for example, are one of lions' worst enemies. With their long shaggy coats and vicious teeth, they're known for their scavenging and sneaky ways – stealing other animals' meals, rather than hunting for their own. They are sly, untrustworthy creatures. I'm sure we all know at least one human who has these traits.

Hyenas, with their vicious teeth, are known for their sneaky ways.

The hyena is known for its eerie laughing sound which really isn't a laugh at all. It is a fake sound that distracts you before you get bitten or before it runs away. Hyenas love to take advantage, and will steal your food if you look the other way. If you have even one hyena around you, you're likely to end up getting bitten. If you there's more than one, they may even be overpowered … Hyenas are in your personal life – those people who make fun of you, try to put you down, try to kill your dreams, be negative about your ideas. They exist in business and property – the people who negatively comment online about what you do, leave you an unnecessary bad review or badmouth your product or service to others. They are in the gym – looking down on you because you don't look as good as they do or you're not as fit or as strong as them. They definitely exist in your relationships – there are unfortunately many people out there who are sly and untrustworthy in relationships. Most of us can definitely relate to one of more of these points. We've all met a few hyenas in our lives.

Sloths are so much cuter than hyenas.
But looks can be deceptive.

Sloths, on the other hand, seem to be the complete opposite of hyenas. They have a reputation for being gentle – with their huge eyes and flat bodies. They are so much cuter than hyenas. But looks can be deceptive. So you may want to avoid them nevertheless, but for different reasons.

Sloths are the slowest mammal on the planet – crawling only one foot per minute when they are on the ground. Their long claws are great for trees, but they find it almost impossible to walk on land, and they sleep for up to 20 hours per day. Their faces always look like they're smiling – even when they are in pain, stressed or anxious. So you never know 100% where you stand with them or what they are thinking. They are slow with just about everything they do – it takes them 30 days to digest a single leaf. They never really achieve much in any part of their lives. They just get by: just earn enough to survive, just eat enough to survive or just remain healthy enough to survive – basically, they live a very basic life. Although they may be content, in my opinion, they don't really know what life is about. I'm sure you've met a few sloths in your time. I know I certainly have.

If you have a sloth around you, it is likely to be a very one-sided relationship as you are likely to end up carrying them. They are unlikely to give back anything back in return.

You're likely to end up carrying a sloth and not getting anything back in return.

My aim in this book is to teach you how to become a mighty lion so that you can succeed in all areas of your life – in business, real estate, your health and relationships.

You don't need to read this book in order. You can jump straight to the section that applies to the area of your life that you want to change. So feel free to go to the section that's most relevant to you. I do recommend however, that you read the whole book afterwards (in whatever order), so that you can get the most from my tips and strategies.

Don't just read this book, study it. Study it like you would a book you had to complete a test on and if you passed you'd win £1 million. If you master the skills in this book, in my opinion, you will be inspired so much that you will change your life for the better in many, many ways. Get yourself a highlighter pen and use it to underline everything on the page that resonates or relates to your current situation. Then, if you ever need a short burst of motivation or a reminder of how to be aligned in business, you can just flick back through the highlighted parts. This way, you're more likely to remember everything I share with you.

Inevitably in life, there will always be hyenas that come snapping at your heels with their negativity or sloths that try to cling to your neck and weigh you down. My aim is to teach you how to think like a lion so you can achieve your dreams and be the best you can be.

WHAT INSPIRED ME TO WRITE THIS BOOK?

I have seven businesses at the moment. I've got a life insurance and mortgage brokers. I've got a company that manages refurbishments of properties: we manage my own properties and the tenants and guests; we source investments for selected clients; plus multiple companies where I hold properties. So, currently, there are seven limited companies. By the time I have released this book, there will probably be more …

Bespoke Financial is the main company which I set up in 2014, and we're the biggest life insurance brokers in the UK now. With over 100 people working for the business across the country, we have won 15 national awards and countless prizes and certificates for our business efforts and results. The five property companies are SPVs (Special Purpose Vehicles) where I hold buy-to-lets, HMOs, serviced accommodation; I've also got a couple of mini hotels. I buy properties, refurbish them, increase their value, re-mortgage, release the funds and then rent them out. So the BRR (Buy, Refurb, Rent) model is everything that I do. There is in excess of £6 million worth of property which I have purchased in just over 3 years from scratch. I've done this whilst having a happy relationship, being a dad and supporting my children, keeping fit, eating well and still having plenty of time off, having 5+ holidays per year (pre-Covid that is), spending time with friends and family and living a balanced, happy and healthy life.

I was inspired to write this book because of my own journey. I wasn't born with a silver spoon in my mouth. Yet through dedication and hard work I have achieved a lot in my life in a short period of time – setting up multiple businesses and winning numerous awards. And my success continues to grow.

When I first started out, I thought it was impossible to have success in all areas of my life. I thought I had to pick and choose what I would be good at. I could be happy in relationships but not a success in business. Or I could be successful in business but not have time for health and fitness.

I realise now that was completely the wrong mindset. So I hope that I can inspire you, but also shave years off your learning curve.

You see, a lot of people think they can only have success in one part of their lives – for example, they can be successful professionally, but they can't be fit or they can't have a successful relationship because they have to work 18 hours a day. Or some people feel that if they're really fit and healthy, they won't have time to run a business. Or they might be employed by somebody else and they believe that they're stuck in that rut of just working 9-to-5 and they'll never get ahead.

I used to think like this too. So I hope that my message will be an inspiration to you. You see, you can have everything that you want in all areas of your life. Thinking that you can't, is just a limiting belief. I hope that after reading my story, and knowing that I am a real person (unlike the majority of plonkers on social media who brag about what they do in business and property and half the time it's a complete lie), and knowing that these are real-life events, this will inspire you.

I haven't been gifted everything as you'll discover when I share a little of my life story with you. I've just worked hard consistently for a good period of time to get to where I am. Now, I just want to get this message out there and to hopefully inspire as many people as possible.

BE A LION IN YOUR LIFE

What I love about lions is that they don't have any limits or restrictions. They don't think, *I'm only going to eat one zebra today.* If they see prey and they're hungry, they'll go for it. They don't have self-doubt. Lions don't think, *Oh, I don't think I can chase that gazelle, it's too fast for me.* They just have a go – even if they fail.

So, for me, becoming a lion is about living a life with no limits, restrictions or fear. By choosing to be a lion, I believe I have that life.

Becoming a lion is about living a life with no limits, restrictions or fear.

To give you an example: seven and a half years ago when I set up my business, I had zero pounds in turnover and we'd done zero sales in life insurance. Now, we are generating millions and millions of pounds in commissions and we're doing over 1000 life insurance policies per month as a company, which I understand is probably the biggest ever number of sales in the history of our industry.

Once I hit that target of 1000 sales in a month, I was challenged to do 10,000 sales a month. I could have said, "I don't know how to do that." But I didn't. Because I have a lion's mindset, I don't have any fear when it comes to big goals. I thought, *Let's go for it.*

It's not because I think I'm better than everybody else; I just don't doubt myself in any way. I think if I put my mind to something and I really go for it, I can achieve absolutely anything. I hope that if you are reading this book, you can think like that, too, or give yourself a little bit more credit or self-belief, because I'm no different to you.

I'm certainly not the best or the richest or the most intelligent. What I am is just someone who goes to work without fear or self-doubt or restrictions. I'll work hard and keep progressing and evolving as much as I can and, because I think like a lion, I won't stop.

Everybody has self-doubt, everybody has challenges in their life. It's how you react to this adversity that matters; whether you let it crush you or push yourself past it and become a better version of yourself. If you said to me 11 years ago that I'd be worth what I'm worth and the size of the business that I've got, I would have laughed at you and said, "There's no way." All I wanted when I was 19 was £50,000 per year. I would never have even contemplated £200,000 £300,000, £400,000 and however many million in assets. My point is: by going through adversity and challenges, then evolving and progressing as a person, you get there eventually.

WHO AM I AND WHY SHOULD YOU LISTEN TO ME?

MY CHILDHOOD

I was about two or three when my parents split up. My dad didn't give my mum any financial support for a good few years. It was just me and her for a long period of time. It must have been so hard for her. I grew up in a rough part of Newcastle, living in a block of flats. I remember when I was younger walking down dirty stairs littered with rubbish and god knows what on the floor, noise coming from different parts of the block. People were taking drugs, fighting, shouting and screaming at all times of night. I remember it well.

My mum and I lived in a block of flats about five or six storeys high and there were loads of rows of these flats. The flats formed a U-shape with a bit of grass at the back. There were always people drinking and getting up to all sorts of trouble. We had a little Jack Russell as a pet, and we took it out for a walk in this yard, and it got mauled by a big Pitbull Staffie. I remember my mum just saying, "Run back in." It was pretty brutal at times.

I was never allowed to play outside by myself, which speaks volumes about the area. I was always told just to play inside. I had a friend in the flat opposite, so I played with her inside the flat because my mum didn't think it was safe to go out.

The one thing I remember well is not having much. I didn't have any entrepreneurial thoughts back then: I was just a kid. I remember life being hard. I didn't really know that we didn't have much money. I just remember being at school and other kids having better coats and shoes than me.

Our street was pretty rough at night. There was always shouting, but it was probably normalised to me because I didn't know any different. The kids I knocked about with back then were probably rough as well.

We moved away from there when I was about eight. My mum set up a recruitment business and was starting to do okay financially. So at Christmas, I started to get presents and things that I wanted for a change. She bought quite a nice house, not a huge house, but it was mega to me compared to what we were used to.

Then, my mum's business folded in 2008 because of the recession. I remember my mum telling me, "We're not going to be able to have all these nice things anymore. You're not going to be able to get as much for Christmas." I remember her working a lot and not really seeing much of her at that point because she was always working. Looking back, she was probably just trying her best to provide as much she could. And she did always provide for me the best she could and is a great mum – so, thank you for that if you're reading this Mum …

So I grew up having nothing, then having something, and then having it taken away again. That had a big influence on me.

Now, I push and push and push to become wealthy and successful, but also to safeguard myself so I never lose everything again. This is where property comes in, because you get a passive income – so it doesn't matter if you lose your job or your business folds, you've still got all that passive income from property coming in. It's like a shield, a protection against losing everything.

So, for me, that's another of my drivers: to get so successful, make so much money and buy so many properties that you get to a stage you couldn't really lose it all. I use my past to motivate me in my present. My drivers keep me motivated when things get tough.

Think about this for a moment. What are your drivers? Is there anything that's happened in your past or in your childhood that still motivates you today?

> **I use my past to motivate me in my present.**
>
> **My drivers keep me motivated when things get tough.**
>
> **What are your drivers?**

My mum did what she could: she even worked a couple of jobs to provide for us. After school, pretty much every day, I would go to my grandma's or the child minder's. I normally had tea there, then got home and went to bed.

When I used to go to school and spoke to other kids, they had been on this holiday or visited that place. They'd done all these things I hadn't done, so only then did I start to realise, *I'm not getting as much as other people.* That just made me really want loads and loads of nice things. I remember really, really wanting it. I never blamed my mum. I didn't think, *Oh, it's her fault that we're in this position,* or anything like that. All I thought was, *I'm going to get all that one day.* That became my goal very early on.

So I had a desire, but I also had a strong belief that I was going to get it as well. Maybe the idea of no-limits came from that time in my life, because although I didn't have anything, I truly believed I would eventually have the things other people had. I used to look at the Argos catalogue and circle all the presents that I wanted. I used to visualise having all those things. I remember looking at how much toys cost. I used to think, *If my mum has made £100,000, then how many toys could that buy? How many Ninja Turtles or Power Rangers?* I remember being really interested in money, what it was, how it was made, what you could do with it.

Now, money isn't the be-all and end-all. Because if you've got no health and you've got loads of money it's irrelevant. However, if you're healthy and you've got a partner and a nice family life and friends, money can make things even better. But back then, I remember just thinking in simple terms of, *Money will get me everything that I want, so I have to make lots of it.*

Remembering those times when everybody else had so much and I didn't, shaped me as an adult. Now, I have a clear idea of things I want in my life. *I want to be happy and healthy. i want nice clothes. I want to have a business that provides me with enough money for a good quality of life. I want enough property so I never have to work again if I choose not to. I want to have a strong mindset. I want to have a happy family. I want good kids. I want a strong relationship. I want a nice home. I want to go on nice holidays and have fun etc, etc I could go on …*

I don't just want some of these things. I want all of it. And so should you. Don't believe anyone who says you can't have everything. You can. What's more, you can have it all if you learn to think like a lion and avoid the hyenas and the sloths. If you imagine life is in a catalogue, you can turn through the pages and circle everything you want: the lifestyle, the body, the business, the partner, the personality, the house. Circle everything you want, and just go and get it. You can choose what your life looks like and how you live it …

You can have it all if you learn to think like a lion and avoid the hyenas and the sloths.

I learned about setting up your own business early on, because my mum set up a recruitment agency where she found construction workers for a big building company. They would need, say, 20 joiners for six weeks, and she would go and find the joiners for them. So it was like a temporary recruitment service for the construction industry. She would find the people, the firm would pay her and she would take commission. The more people she recruited, the more money she made.

So, she was incentivised to go to construction firms and say, "Instead of taking people on and employing them full-time, we'll do your temporary contracts for you." She then sourced all of the trades and she made really good money doing that.

I remember being interested in this and asking, "How does it work, Mum? How have you got all this? How have you bought this computer for me for Christmas?" I remember our phone constantly ringing – Saturdays, Sundays, late at night. Then she used to go into a different room, speak for a bit, come back, go into a different room again. That gave me the work ethic.

I remember asking, "How does the business work? How do we have money now? How do you get paid from it?" I was fascinated with how much money people could make. I remember asking her, "How much money do you make? How does that work? How much do the construction companies make? How much do your staff make?" I was always interested in how much money people made for doing different things.

Seeing her going to work all the time gave me a good work ethic and I also understood that a lot of her success was because of her business.

Then in 2008, things went horribly wrong. How it worked was that these big construction companies wouldn't pay for 90 days. They might need 20 joiners for six months at £20 an hour. In the meantime, my mum had to pay them weekly out of her own pocket before she would be paid by the construction firms. There was a factoring company that lent my mum the money to pay the trades, but then she had to wait 90 days for the cash to come in to pay the factoring company back.

Obviously, with hindsight, you can see that's not the best business model because of the time delay after payment upfront. It worked while the economy was great. But then 2008 happened. She'd already paid the trades something like £180,000 in wages, but then the firm they were working for went bust. She'd already borrowed the money from the factoring company, so then she also had to go bust. It wasn't even her own fault.

I remember her telling me, "We're going to have to move out of the house," and, "It's not going to be like it has been at Christmas." I kind of understood, but I also didn't. I wondered, *Well, why?* In spite of this though I always had the faith and belief that, *It'll come back. We'll get it all back again.*

I started to rebel when I got into middle school. I really struggled with taking orders and being told what to do, so I was very argumentative with teachers to a point where I would stubbornly refuse to do as I was told.

It must have been horrible to try and teach me, because everything that they said, I would do the opposite or point-blank refuse. They would put me on detention or suspend me, but I still refused to cooperate. I didn't get on with any teachers in middle school and high school. They used to tell me constantly that I was never going to achieve anything.

I got separated from a lot of my friends in class, because the teachers thought I was a bad influence. Parents used to scowl at me in the playground, because they thought I was leading their son or daughter astray. I remember a time—it must have been horrible for my mum—when I was 12 at the school disco. I was drinking vodka and smoking weed, being sick all over the toilets. I'd been sick in the sink and the headmaster had to come and unplug the sink. So they rang my mum and she had to drag me home which led to all the other parents tutting and shaking their heads about us. That must have been so embarrassing for her. I was a bit of a loose cannon.

From about 12 to 16, I was a nightmare—getting up to all sorts of stupid things. I was with the wrong crowd. I was taking drugs and drinking heavily. I kind of went off the boil and failed everything. My mum would tell me, "You need to be in at this time." But I used to stay out all hours and go missing for the day. My mum would be driving round the streets looking for me because I used to turn my phone off. With hindsight, that must have been horrible for her.

I moved out aged 16, two weeks after I finished school, into my own flat. That time is all a bit of a blur now, because I was taking drugs and drinking so much.

I lived in this dingy bedsit. It was dirty and disgusting. The living room and the bedroom were in the same room with a tiny little kitchen and bathroom that were horrible. Upstairs were druggies. Downstairs were druggies. Across the way were druggies. There was constant partying until three o'clock in the morning. At four o'clock, it was also boom, boom, boom! Music was blasting all of the time. I was hardly getting any sleep in this environment.

I was a joiner/carpenter from 16 to 19. Close towards the end of school, my mum sat me down and asked, "What do you want to do?" I didn't know. I didn't like anything at school. I didn't have any hobbies. I didn't have a clue what I wanted to do. So she said, "Right, well, you're going into construction. You're getting a trade. That's a good job." Because she had a construction background, she helped to give me a start. So I was just nudged into it as I didn't know what else I wanted to do.

I soon discovered that when you're an apprentice joiner, you're just basically the dogsbody. People will say, "Go make the tea. Go make the coffee. Go and pick up all that wood and move it over there." You get the worst of the worst jobs—like unblocking drains—and you're treated like a nobody. You're treated badly because you're the apprentice. The older people who work on building sites would say, "When I was an apprentice, you had to make the tea. That's what you've got to do for two years."

I was very argumentative. As an apprentice, you have to work with a squad of joiners, so I worked with two joiners at the start. They used to say, "Make the tea," and I would say, "No, you make the tea." They'd reply, "But you're the apprentice. You have to." "Well, I'm not bothered. I don't want a cup of tea, so I'm not making one." They bullied me a little bit because there were grown men and I was a skinny 16-year-old fresh from school. So I ended up still making the tea sometimes, even though I would argue with them. Then, because I pushed back, they gave me the shittest of the shit jobs: like standing in the pouring rain building a fence or similar. I kept being moved from building site to building site, and working with different joiners, because I was so argumentative. I didn't like authority, being ordered about and having no control over my life.

Half of the people I worked with had dodgy backs, dodgy shoulders, dodgy elbows, dodgy knees from working so hard and putting strain on their body, which is what construction does. I remember saying to them, "I'm not going to be doing this forever, you know." They'd reply, "Yeah, yeah, we said that 40 years ago. Everyone thinks like that. You'll be doing this for the next 50 years, young'un. This is all you're going to be doing now." I'd say, "No, I won't." "Well, we used to think that as well, but you've just got to crack on. You've just got to do your job, get your house, get a nice missus, have a couple of kids and have a good life."

I used to think, *Fuck that. I'm not doing that. Not for me.* I used to have this little voice that would rear its head every once in a while, this self-belief. I would say, "I'm going to be a millionaire: I'm going to do something massive in my life." They would just laugh: "Oh yeah, of course you are. How are you going to do that? What are you going to do?" I'd reply: "I don't know, but I am going to." They used to really put me down and say I was full of shit.

But rather than pull me down, that motivated me because I used to think, *You know what, fuck them. I'm definitely doing this and I'm going to prove every single one of them wrong: all the teachers, everyone at work, everybody.*

Once you've finished your apprenticeship, you would normally either be offered a full-time job or you would have to leave, basically because you're not good enough and they don't want you. So I had to leave the second my apprenticeship was over, because I think I just annoyed everyone.

After I lost my job as a joiner, I decided to drown my sorrows so I went drinking for about two weeks, behaving like an idiot. I remember being out from the Thursday until Sunday. I'd been partying, drinking, taking drugs and doing stupid things for three days straight. I remember on the Sunday looking in the bathroom mirror. My face was sucked in and gaunt and I looked yellow. I just looked ill. I remember looking at myself thinking, *What am I doing? I haven't even enjoyed myself all weekend. The people I'm hanging around with are partying constantly. I need to get out of this life because it's no good for me.*

So, the partying all stopped because I realised, *I'm going nowhere. My life is a mess.* At the age of 19, I then decided to stop all the self-destructive behaviour. I realised: I don't want to go down that path. I thought, *You know what, this has to change now. I need to stop this. I need to sort myself out, get a new career, do something with myself and do something like I was meant to do.*

Then, I started to remember what I used to believe: that I was going to achieve something big and I was going to have everything.

So then I made up a CV and I sent it to loads of places, saying I had loads of experience in loads of different areas. I was offered a sales job for an insurance company, Combined Insurance Company of America.

When I rang my mum and told her I had a job doing self-employed commission-only sales, she said, "Oh no, Terry, you can't do this. It's self-employed, so if you don't make any sales you don't get paid." My grandfather was the same and wanted to stop me. But I had no other options. I didn't like being a joiner. So I put my foot down.

They both laugh about it now. My granddad who is 87 always says, "I'm glad you didn't listen to me. I'm glad you didn't quit." Because then, literally within a couple of weeks, I was earning in a week selling insurance what I used to make in a month of being a joiner. I was making around £60,000 – making £1,000 a week when I used to make £1,000 a month – which was mind-blowing for me at the time.

BECOMING SELF-EMPLOYED

The person who interviewed me had been a bit flash in the interview, showing off his good-looking girlfriend, his £200,000 a year income, his car, and his mansion. He was telling me, "You could be like me. You could have this too."

At the time, he was what I wanted to be like. He gave me the impression that he had everything in every part of his life. He wasn't speaking down to me. He was telling me, "This is how you do it. This is how you sell. These are the products. This is what you do. You can have this too."

The first couple of weeks I was working for the company, I smashed it. They had leader boards and I was at the top. We used to have morning meetings and people would ask, "Who is this Terry guy?" I used to come in and all the guys who were 40 to 50 years old, were asking me, "How are you getting those scores? How are you selling? What do you do?"

So I had stopped being around hyenas and sloths. I was finally with people who thought like I did. I thought, *People think I'm good at this. This is a nice feeling. I like this. I like being admired and having the recognition.* Because I was definitely not the best at school; I was never the top at anything. Now, all of a sudden, I was the top at life insurance sales and I felt like, *Fucking hell, this is amazing.* So I got addicted to that feeling of being at the top.

Because I was so young and everybody else on that team was 40+, they all took me under their wing. It was the complete opposite of the people I'd worked with when I was a joiner when they put me down, gave me the worst jobs and acted like I was beneath them. Now, all of a sudden there were older people who were putting me on a pedestal and treating me like I was the next big thing, saying, "No one does what you're doing at your age. How on earth are you doing all this? You're amazing. Do you know what you're going to achieve in your life if you're doing this at 19?" I was stunned to be thought so well of and to be so good at something.

At that time, I wasn't thinking about property or long-term wealth creation. I just had tunnel vision—sell as much as I could to make as much money as I could.

So, at the beginning it was "make money, money, money" that was the driver. Then, it almost became just solely about being top. I felt, *I want to be top no matter what.* The money was just a by-product of being top of the leader boards.

So I sold my joinery tools after the first or second week. It was a couple of thousand pounds' worth of tools and I sold them all. My mum and granddad asked if I was sure what I was doing. But I was certain. I said, "I am never going back to sawing wood and hammering nails ever again." Looking back, that was probably a bit of a rash thing to do, because in reality a lot of people do have a good start in self-employed sales, then they dip off. But I never did go back to being a joiner. Nor did my sales ever dip!

It was pretty brutal in my new job. I was walking into shops, knocking on doors, selling life insurance. It's not like I had a tangible physical product to sell. I wasn't selling laptops or cars: I was selling a product that was not there.

What's more, it's hard to sell life insurance, because nobody wants to think about dying and or getting cancer. Loads of people put it off or think life insurance is a con.

So, I was selling to them a vision of, "If you die, you need to make sure that your children are looked after and the only way to do that is life insurance if you don't have savings." I would go as far as saying it's one of the hardest sales roles that there is: selling life insurance with no leads. I had to generate every client that I ever had. We were finding 12 to 15 new clients a week by cold-calling. Anybody who has cold-called before knows how hard that is.

We used to have a morning meeting in the Marriott Hotel in Gosforth, Newcastle. We'd have a meeting and then we used to stand on our chairs and sing *Zip-a-Dee-Doo-Dah Zip-a-Dee-Ay*. It was very American— so there was lots of singing and shouting. What I didn't know at the time was that we were doing affirmations.

We would shout: "I am happy, I am healthy, I am terrific." We used to do that every day. I would think, *These people are mad. What are these 40-year-old men doing standing on chairs?* But I would think, *Fuck it, I'll just get on with it and join in!*

Then, they would say, "Right, Terry, you're in Cramlington today," or "You're in Blythe today." We used to literally go down the high street with our folders and walk into every single shop and pitch the owner life insurance. We used to have a script that we followed for every person. So I used to get told, "Piss off, get out of my shop" and I was thrown out of multiple shops. This was during the day from 9am to 5pm. Then, from 5pm to 9pm each night, I used to knock on doors when people got in from work. So I was working crazy hours

– 12 hours a day, five or six days a week. I was still a teenager and I was hearing lots of negatives: "No." "Piss off." "Fuck off." "Get out of my shop." "Get out of my face." "You're a conman." People would say all sorts of horrible things.

But I'd never done sales before, so I just thought, *This is what sales is like.* Everyone at that company had the attitude of, "Oh, that's what happens. That's what people do." So I just thought that was normal.

Then, I started getting results by smiling when people opened the door, by having a chat, making them laugh or just being nice. People do seem to like me and warm to me, so I think that's why I've probably done so well at sales. When I was knocking on doors, I wasn't a 50-year-old in a pinstripe suit with grey hair who was trying to just push a product on them. Maybe they looked at me and thought, *Oh, he's new. He looks young. We'll help him out.* Because at that time life insurance was dominated by middle-aged men.

I was a bit naïve maybe at that age; I didn't really know any different. When I got that taste for being Number 1, I felt like, *I'm having this every week now, no matter what.* The league table used to come out sometimes midweek. So on Wednesday, I would be thinking, *Oh, I'm behind. I'm just going to work more now.* I was literally knocking on people's doors sometimes at 10pm at night.

Then, I started to get referrals. When I sold to somebody, I used to ask them to refer me to their friends and family – then, I used to go and see them. So it got easier. If you get referrals, you don't have to cold call as much.

My life was completely out of balance back then. My first thoughts were all about work. I slacked off at the gym; I wasn't training. I was out from 8am till 10pm at night. I didn't see my partner: I used to get in and she was already asleep, so I went to sleep after her. I was up from the same time as her, but then it was breakfast and I was quickly out of the door.

That was five or six days a week and it definitely broke down that relationship, because I was working so much. However, the pleasure I was getting from winning all the awards and achieving a lot, led to me thinking, *Well, fuck everything else. This is what I want to do.*

I see now that's definitely not the right way of thinking. But back then, it was the first time I had found a career I loved and I was making good money. So I didn't mind sacrificing other things to achieve that success.

Maybe you can relate that? When you start your career or a business, you tend to neglect everything else. To a degree, you maybe even need to do that to get ahead. But eventually you realise that you need to get some balance because there's no point being wealthy but having no one to spend it on or having loads of money but being really unhealthy.

The high points for me during this time were the recognition and the trophies: being Number 1 in the North East, Number 1 nationally. I won a weekend away in the Lake District where we went on a boat trip with all the top performers across the UK. I turned up in a tee-shirt while everybody else was in suits, because I'd never been on anything like that before. Yet everyone was so welcoming and full of praise.

All I used to think about was being Number 1 and the very best at what I was doing. I remember going up to the top guy who was running the American business then and telling him, "I'll be the biggest thing this industry has ever seen. I'm going to run this whole industry in years to come, just you watch."

People didn't put me down like the joiners. Instead, they were encouraging and would say, "Yes, I'm sure you will." I felt at home. I started to think, *There are people who are like me – all really determined to make money.* A lot of the top salespeople across the country were similar to me. They thought the same; they acted the same. I felt at home.

So, when I got to Number 1, I thought, *I want to stay here, but I need to make a mark. I want to make history. I want to be the best of all time – ever – in financial services.* And that is exactly what I have achieved.

Combined Insurance Company of America went bust, and then I went to MetLife Europe. At MetLife Europe I was the youngest ever sales manager in their history at the age of 23.

But there were loads of restrictions at MetLife about what you could and couldn't do, which I found frustrating. So I spoke to my best mate, Lee Flanagan, and suggested setting up our own business. I said, "If we just set up ourselves, we could have a direct relationship with Aviva, Legal & General, AIG, all of the insurance companies. Then, we could offer clients more, which would mean we'd sell more. We could build our teams quicker and better."

So, we set it up in partnership in June 2014. Again, when we joined this network, called First Complete at the time – now called PRIMIS – there were loads of people doing loads more business than us.

At the time, Lee and I said to everyone, "We will be the top in this network." I actually have a video from six years ago where I stood up and told the audience, "We're going to run this network. We're going to be the biggest. We're going to beat all of you on the leader boards – trust me." Their attitude was, "Yeah, right. What, you young kids coming in here selling life insurance, when we've been doing it 25 years? No, you're not."

It was a battle, but we got there within five years. Right now my business is Number 1 in the country in our network. In the UK, in our mortgage network, there are a couple of thousand businesses and we're Number 1 by a mile on insurance sales.

SETTING UP MY FIRST BUSINESS

The process of setting up a business was challenging. There was a lot to learn and I made a lot of mistakes. I had to self-educate myself on business and what to do. At big events, dinners and conventions, I intentionally used to sit beside the top people in the network, the people who were achieving the most, and I would ask them, "How do you do this? How do you do that?"

I was like a sponge: I used to soak up all the information, then implement it. They weren't telling me, "You must do this or that." It was more, "This is how I do it." When someone says that to me, I will then look at it and ask, *Okay, so could I use that or not? Could I put my own spin on that? Would that work for me?* If I think it will be useful to me, I'll then implement it and run with it.

That's how I progressed so quickly: learning from other people, being willing to learn from my mistakes, and having a crazy work ethic. I was initially working stupid hours every day, every week and every month.

When I first set it up, all of a sudden I had more money than I have ever had before and I was a little reckless with it. I was not buying big cars or anything crazy like that, but I wasn't watching the bottom line enough. I was just focusing on the top line as in, *Let's bring in as many sales as I possibly can.* I wasn't focusing on what was going out, the expenditure, or looking at profits and losses. This is something I learned more about as time went on.

Most of my success came from my dedication to educating myself. I don't watch TV or play any sport. I don't have any other hobbies. So, for a long time I used to get up in the morning, do my exercise, work all day relentlessly, get in, have some food, watch motivational videos on how to sell and how to run a business, go to sleep, repeat.

I was absolutely obsessed with it and I think that passion got me through the hard times at the start. We're very fortunate to live in the Age that we do, because you can find out anything on YouTube pretty much and there are lots of other people sharing their knowledge. You can learn from other people's mistakes instead of your making own, by listening and then backing it up with action.

If I watch something and think, *That's good, I could use that*, I will take action right away. I will do it. Whereas I know plenty of people who are well-educated and spend £20,000 on a training course. They might know everything about investing in buy-to-lets. But they never take any action. Without action, knowledge and training is absolutely pointless. You have to be good at taking huge action whenever you are given an idea.

For me, when someone successful says, "This is how I run my business," if I respect and look up to this person, I'll also do it myself.

I used to think networking events were a waste of time because I used to think, *Why would I want to go to an event, chat with loads of people and pretend to be interested in them, when I really just want their business?* That's essentially what networking is: people are going because they want business from you, not because they want to be your friend. That's the way I used to look at it.

Now, I understand that networking is a way of meeting like-minded people and sharing knowledge. I am at a stage where I feel like I want to help people if I can and share my experience. A lot of people shared their knowledge with me in the past and gave me advice when I asked for it. So if anyone asks me for advice, I want to help them if I can. It's about giving back – which is also why I'm writing this book.

BE A LION:

IN BUSINESS

CONNECT WITH ME

Take pictures of your journey as a lion – include photos of yourself; sections of this book that you find helpful; quotes that you like; your list of goals, etc. Then, post it and tag me on Instagram.

THE BUSINESS WILDERNESS

The business wilderness consists of the following animals:

Lions

People who set up multiple successful businesses, making fortunes, with huge happy teams – everything they touch turns to gold. They are progressing constantly, winning awards and moving to new levels each year. They feast on fresh meat every day

Hyenas

People who say: "Businesses are too risky," "You could go bankrupt and lose everything," "Get a steady job – it's safer," "You can't run a business, you're not good enough or experienced enough." They are negative about your dreams and put you down. No matter what you do achieve or say, they have a smart answer as to why you're wrong or doing the wrong thing.

Sloths

People who don't even know how business works, don't have enough energy or motivation to set up anything. They just want their pay cheque each month to pay the bills and get by.

WHY WOULD YOU WANT YOUR OWN BUSINESS?

With a job there is the 40/40/40 rule – most people will work 40 hours a week for 40 years of their life and then only end up with 40 percent of the income that they earned, because they'll get taxed on the rest. Why would you be in that situation: getting taxed 60 percent and ending up with 40 percent left of your income?

You'll never get taxed that much if you're self-employed or you structure it through a limited company, so there are huge tax advantages to setting up your own business or working for yourself.

You're in control of your own destiny. You can write your own pay cheque instead of relying on someone else to write it for you. You don't have to request your holidays. You can holiday when you want, work when you want, where you want, recruit the right people that you want around you.

Self-doubt is like a hyena snapping its teeth at you.

A lot of people who are employed complain about their colleagues saying: "This person does this and this person does that" or "The company would do so much better without him or her." You can choose who you work with when you run your own business – both clients and staff!

You can also make a hell of a lot more money, which then enables you to invest more in property and other investment vehicles.

The benefits of having your own business:

- Huge tax advantages.
- In control of your own destiny.

- Holiday when you want, without permission.
- Work when and where you want.
- Work with people you like and want to work with.
- Don't have to wait for someone else to give you a promotion.
- You are the boss.
- Make more money – which allows you to make other investments.

It's just a shift of mindset to work for yourself. Ultimately, everybody is self-employed – because if you're employed on a salary and you don't go to work at the time you're meant to each day, you don't get paid. Being self-employed is exactly the same. If you don't go to work and do what you're meant to do, you're not going to get paid. So, at the end of the day everybody is 'self-employed'. They just look at it differently.

Loads of people say, "I need a salary. I need the security. I need to know what's coming in every month." Again that's a mindset thing. For a start, your job is always dependent on the business you're working for doing well. So that means if that business starts struggling, you could be made redundant or lose your job. And why do you need to know how much money is coming in? You may know £2000 is coming in, but that's all that's going to come in. You are limited to that amount every month unless you get a pay rise, even if your food and energy bills keep going up – which actually means you're taking a pay cut. So you're limiting yourself by saying, "I need that much coming in each month."

So again, it's about mindset. It's about confidence. Some people think, *What happens if I don't make enough money?* They're doubting themselves. That's the self-doubt of the hyena snapping its teeth at them. It's the hyena snarling, "You can't do this. You can't do that. What happens if you don't make enough money?" You're thinking like an animal that looks to take food off other animals, rather than hunting down food for itself. So it's all self-doubt.

A hyena will snarl and tell you, "You can't do this. You can't do that."

With most employed jobs, people just tick along and get by. They live pay cheque to pay cheque and often they never really achieve anything lasting or meaningful. They get in at 9am and they clockwatch and wish their life away until 5pm. At five seconds past 5pm, they rush out of the door and normally go and do the same mundane things: watch TV, eat, go to sleep, repeat. They're just doing the same things over and over again. All their hard work is benefiting someone else.

At the end of the day, if you do what average people do, take an average job, work an average 40-hour week, you're going to get an average satisfaction, average holidays, and average income which determines the quality of your life.

You have the choice whether to do this or not – whether you want to accept that you're going to be like everyone else or you're going to be different and control your own destiny and your family's destiny by doing something different.

You have a choice.

Avoid thinking like a hyena that looks to snatch food off other animals, rather than hunting food for itself.

The main message I would like to get across in this book is: you can do it. You don't have to be really academically intelligent. You don't have to be special or unbelievably talented. The starting point is believing that you can do it—you can have a business and everything else you want in life.

CHALLENGE OR OPPORTUNITY?

Sometimes things that seem like difficult challenges at the time turn out to be for the best. There was no light bulb moment for me when I decided to leave my joiner's job and become self-employed.

I did it because I got made redundant as a joiner, so I had no job. I applied for everything and it just so happened that I got an offer in self-employed sales. I didn't ever set out to be self-employed.

However, there was no doubt in my mind when I was offered this position. I wasn't thinking, *Oh, what happens if I don't get paid? What happens if I can't cover my bills? What happens if no one buys off me?* Those thoughts didn't once enter my head. I was only focusing on the opportunity, on the positives – not the negatives. So, I was thinking, *Right, so I just follow this process. I have to sell life insurance to this many people in order to make this much money.* Maybe that's because I was so young: I just didn't have self-doubt or fear.

Setting up my own business beyond self-employment was a natural extension of that. I didn't have any fear about that. I didn't think I couldn't do it. There were no hyenas around to give me self-doubt. It was just that lion mindset of, *I'm going to do this, and when I do it I'm going to be the best at it and I'm going to dominate it and I'm going to run it the way I want it to be run.*

The lion's mindset is: I'm going to dominate.

I always look on the positive side and have a 'cup half full' mindset. Don't get me wrong: I still look at some of the negatives but I won't let myself focus on them for too long. If I look at something and think, *Oh well, there's a downside of this,* then I will instantly think, *What's the solution?* With every downside, there's a solution.

So, if you don't sell, you don't get paid. Yes, but if you sell loads you get paid loads, so you have a bigger motivation to work hard. There's an upside to every downside. That's just the way I look at things. That's the lion's mindset.

It's similar with property investment. I hear people say, "What happens if you get bad tenants and they break the boiler? What happens if they don't pay the rent? What happens if they trash the house?" That's the hyena mindset. What happens if they don't? What happens if you get a tenant who stays in the property for 10 years and takes care of it like it's their own home? There are two sides to every situation. It depends on what you look at, how you look at it, what you focus on, and what you believe. It all begins and ends with having the right kind of mindset.

There's an upside to every downside.
That's the lion's mindset.

ARE YOU CUT OUT FOR BUSINESS?

I strongly disagree with all these online training companies saying, "Leave your job and start a business." It's not a one size fits all. You can't say that for everybody. Yes, for some people it might be right, but for some people it's definitely wrong. So, therefore, I feel it's bad advice to tell you to leave your job without weighing up the pros and cons first and assessing if this is right for you.

At the end of the day, everybody's situation is different so it would be foolish to leave your high-paying job to start a business without asking yourself some tough questions first.

Firstly, have you got savings? Have you got a cushion? Realistically, you need at least 6 to 12 months' expenditure in the bank or a passive income before you would leave your job. Don't just jump into it without a financial cushion.

But again there are variables to everything, because if you're a young person with no mortgage, no partner, no kids, living with your parents, you could easily quit your job and you're not going to get into that much financial difficulty. If you're someone who's got three kids and a mortgage and you're the main earner in the household, you have different responsibilities and priorities. So, it's probably not the best decision without thinking it through carefully.

The decision depends on you, the type of business you want to set up, and your personal situation, too.

Although the lion mindset is to have no limits, no fear, and be confident in yourself and your ability, that does not mean being reckless and foolish. You can still be calculated when you do this – don't put yourself and your family at risk by making a rash decision. Timing in most areas of life is very important.

With everything in life, I believe you should enjoy what you're doing. What do they say: work is two-thirds of your life or something crazy? Work is a huge part of your life – you can't escape that. So why not do something that you enjoy? If you don't, then change it!

If you want to be a sloth and just tick along, that's fine. But don't expect all the financial rewards and the amazing life that comes with them. Don't expect to be achieving huge things. You'll just be hanging in the tree watching while others are having that life instead of you.

If you want to be a sloth, that's fine.
But don't expect all the financial rewards and the
amazing life.

WHAT IS YOUR PASSION?

Do you know what your passions are? I know some people are 40 to 50 years old and they still don't know what their true passion is. They still haven't found out what they truly enjoy or what sets them on fire. I think that's sad. You should never do anything for money alone, because you can only get so far by just doing something for money without any passion.

A good example of someone fired up with passion is Alfie Best who I just interviewed for my podcast "The Rags to Riches Show with

Terry Blackburn" – available on Apple podcast and Spotify if you want to listen to it. Alfie owns Wyldecrest Parks: a hundred mobile home sites with 16,000 tenants and £750 million in property assets. He told me his business only got so far when he was just focusing on money. The second he shifted his focus from money to providing a great quality service for people who want to live in mobile homes, his business really flourished. Alfie was brought up as a gypsy and lived in a caravan growing up which makes his achievements even more impressive. He is passionate about providing a good quality service and mobile homes for people to live in and have holidays in. It's because of his passion that his business has flourished. He became a billionaire within 20 years.

THERE IS NO OVERNIGHT SUCCESS

It's important to realise that there is no such thing as "overnight success" in business. People often look on Instagram and Facebook and see these amazing lives that people are leading – often, there are years and years and years of hard work going on in the background to get to where they are today. If it's happened "overnight" I'd question if it is actually real – unfortunately, there are a lot of bluffers and blaggers online, so don't believe most of what you see.

Of course, everybody wants success yesterday, for free. They don't want to pay the price or even half the price that the people have paid who are achieving these things. Sometimes, it's ruined relationships, health, friendships, or multiple parts of their life to get to where they are. Often, they've sacrificed a lot of things, even if it's just nights out with their friends, meals with a partner, seeing their children growing up.

Everybody wants the rewards, but they don't necessarily want to pay the price.

Don't think by setting up a business you're going to be a millionaire next year and you're going to breeze through it. There are still going to be no problems and challenges. If you want it all, there is more often than not a huge price to pay upfront.

THE SHIT STICK ANALOGY

A humorous analogy that I use to illustrate this is: imagine you're walking a dog in a field and you come across a little stick that has a bit of dog shit on the end. If you just want a normal life, it will be like dealing with that stick. It's a little stick and it has a little bit of shit that comes with it – because everybody's life will have some shit at some point, whether it's your partner causing you headaches, children getting into trouble, arguing with friends, work problems, money issues. You'll always have a little bit of shit.

Then, if you venture further down that field where the grass is lusher and greener, you then find there's a massive stick but it has a huge shit farm on the end. Now, this represents the life of a very, very successful businessman. So, on one side he's got everything that he's ever wanted – the massive stick. He's got all the amazing things in life: the holidays, the cars, the big houses, the beautiful woman, the friendships, everything. But on the other side of that massive stick, there is a huge shit farm.

Because the more that you achieve, the bigger everything gets, and the more successful you get, the bigger your problems will be. With a prettier partner there are going to be more blokes that hit on her and try to take her off you. If you become hugely wealthy, there are people who will try to sue you, who will try to mimic you, who will try to drag you down and ruin your business. The bigger you get, the more shit that you have to be prepared to deal with.

So, in summary, there's a little bit of shit on the average stick, but if you want the massive stick with the big amazing life, you've got to be prepared to deal with loads and loads of shit: in fact, a shit farm full of it!

In a 9-to-5 job you don't have HR problems. You don't have people coming to you saying: "Oh, I'm pregnant" or "I'm ill" or "This person said this to me" or "I'm going to take action against you for this reason" or "I'm going to leave" or "I'm going to set up myself and take all your clients off you."

You don't get all that when you're just doing a normal job. But you don't get all the rewards and success that comes with it either. Think about it: what stick do you want to pick up? If it's the big one, you have to prepare yourself for a shit farm.

GETTING STARTED: LAUNCHING YOUR BUSINESS

There's a lot of learn in business. Initially, it's just about getting your house in order. Here are some of the aspects you will need to consider after you have decided on the type of business you're going to start:

- A lot of research and planning prior to doing anything;
- Risks and rewards;
- Soul-searching to determine if this is definitely for you;
- Compliance elements;
- Business banking;

- Making sure you've got the right insurance;
- Liability insurance;
- Employing staff.

Along with the obvious stuff!

Your launch will be different depending on the industry. If you're bringing a product to market, you will have to do product research first. There's a magical thing called Google that has everything you need. You can go on there to do your research.

Another strategy is to find somebody who is doing well in the same space and ask for their advice. You don't have to find out everything yourself: you'll save time if you ask somebody else.

When I first got into life insurance, I went up to all the top salespeople and asked, "How do you close? What's your intro like? What's your sales process like? Which product do you sell most of? Why? What's your typical client profile?" I learned as much as I could from people who were already successful.

Become a sponge and soak up as much information as you can from people who are already doing what you want to do. Write everything down and study it. If you want to set up a social media platform, of course you're not going to get to speak to Mark Zuckerberg. But you can get to speak to somebody else at the top of their game if you message them, ring them, or turn up at their office. If you're determined enough and your mindset is right, you'll find a way to speak to them.

Just make sure that you avoid analysis paralysis, as in you're not just studying and studying and learning and learning and not taking any action. There's a medium somewhere between not knowing enough to get started and knowing so much but not starting! There's a medium where you know enough and you're passionate about it and you think you can do it. So go for it!

STANDING THE TEST OF TIME

Some of the businesses that are topical and preferred right now are those that have a recurring income or a subscription model.

Everyone said that Netflix wouldn't work, but it killed off Blockbuster because it had a subscription model. Blockbuster had an opportunity to buy Netflix, but said, "No – no one will ever pay a subscription." Look what happened after that. Netflix is obviously hugely valuable because it has a subscription that comes in every single month.

Property has the same model: buy-to-lets and HMOs have a recurring income. (Though, obviously, unexpected things can happen: tenants can move out and there may be maintenance or repairs that need to be done.)

Any service-based model where you're providing a monthly service for a subscription is always a good one, ideally as recession-proof as possible.

On the flipside of that, think about the businesses that are going down. Look at what Uber has done to taxi firms. Also, think about developing technology and likely future changes. For example, think about autonomous vehicles. When cars can self-drive fully, they'll eventually kill off Uber because an autonomous car with no driver will go and pick up people, then drop them off at their destination.

Therefore taxi drivers will be gone. So who knows if Uber will survive: they will probably just buy loads of Teslas to get around that. It's anyone's guess. That's just an example of the type of forward-thinking you need to apply: you've got to think about the industries that are likely to be impacted both positively and negatively.

If you look at certain jobs, such as train drivers, there's absolutely no need for them. Trains can drive themselves. At a certain stage on the track, it clicks a switch that then brakes and the train stops in time for the station. Train drivers aren't really needed. Sorry to any train drivers reading this – it's just my opinion. You also don't need a conductor walking up and down the train, because they can be replaced with check-in machines. So those are the types of industries that will change and jobs that will go.

Mechanics are going to be massively hit eventually, because everything is going to go electric. Backstreet garages are likely to be massively hit because there are less things that can go wrong with an electric engine. With time, all cars are going to be electric and there is a growing push for shared cars to reduce emissions and pollution. So certain car manufacturers, unless they evolve, are going to disappear. What will then happen to oil prices, car parts and petrol stations and mechanics who just fix petrol or diesel cars?

These days, houses are being built using a 3-D printer. Traditional housebuilding methods may have changed in the past, but it's always involved humans. Even with the diggers and cranes, people were still needed to operate them. Most houses took about 3 to 9 months to build using traditional methods. But now, industrial 3D printers can create concrete homes based on a 3D model and build them autonomously. So, an entire 3D-printed house can be built in a day! The work can be done faster, more accurately, and more cost-effectively as it uses less materials.

So if lots of houses start to be built like that, what's going to happen to the construction industry? It's not going to go away entirely, because people are always going to need maintenance and want to build the old-fashioned way. But the construction industry is really going to be hit. It's certainly not going to be like it is now.

Lots of industries are going to be impacted as a result of AI and robots. So when you're thinking about setting up or selling a business, don't be in an industry that's likely to disappear.

Another one to consider is books and bookshops. Amazon has just absolutely killed off bookshops because most people are now buying audio and books online.

So try to set up or invest in a business with a subscription model. Consider if your business has longevity – is it in an industry that's going to grow? Does it have a good product or service that's likely to be around for a long time and is going to expand? Or is it a business that's likely to be impacted by new technology? 'Do young people use it now?' is normally a good indicator too.

YOUR BUSINESS NAME

If you're creative, you can probably come up with your business name yourself.

Let me take you through the process that I use myself. I set up another business just the other day: it's another property company for holiday lets. I wanted the word 'luxurious' in the business name but because a lot of people would already thought of that, all variations of property company names including that word were taken (luxurious properties, luxurious holiday lets, luxurious stays etc.). So I typed the word 'luxurious' into an online thesaurus and it gave me all of the different variations for the same word. In this case, I liked the word "heavenly" so I used that as part of the name for one of my companies.

Whatever your business or your message is, you can use an online tool like that just to get different words for the name – it's simple but effective. Then, you can check at Companies' House online to see if the name has already been taken or not. The name needs to be short and snappy. It needs to do what it says on the tin. It also needs to stand out.

There's a great book by Seth Godin called *Purple Cow*. The key message is that if you were to drive along the road past some ordinary cows, you wouldn't tell your friends when you get to your destination, "I've just seen some cows in a field."

But if you drove past a purple cow, you would say, "Bloody hell, I've just seen a purple cow." You'd tell everyone, wouldn't you? The message here is that there are loads of other businesses the same as yours, so it's not going to stand out unless it's a purple cow. People aren't going to remember the same old, same old.

A good example of that is in financial services. In life insurance sales and mortgage brokerages, there are loads of John Smith Financial Solutions etc., where it's somebody's name and it's very basic. They never ever stand out because there are so many of them. Nobody cares who John Smith is when they are looking for mortgage or life insurance. With businesses like this, they put their ego into it or don't seem to have given it a lot of thought.

This is why I chose the name Bespoke Financial for my own business. The definition of "bespoke" is to tailor something specially to suit the individual. That's what we do with our life insurance: we offer bespoke solutions tailored to each individual. So I included this word in our company name because that's what we do for clients. It sounds established and credible.

Some high-net worth individuals ring us up and ask, "Do you offer bespoke finance?" or "Do you offer bespoke financial advice?" "Bespoke" is what they are used to asking for and it means we are speaking their sort of language. So, just the name in itself draws the right kind of people to the business.

Similarly, with my podcast, "The Rags to Riches Show" my audience likes hearing about successful people's life stories and being inspired. It does what it says on the tin.

All of my businesses follow this trend – good solid names and brands that stand out.

The message you give depends on your industry and the type of clients you want to attract. But your name and brand really does matter, especially in the day and age that we're living in.

MAKING SALES

Some people feel daunted by the idea of selling things. They might say, "Oh, I'm not a salesman. I couldn't do sales." Truth is: you are already in "sales". You are selling all day, every day, whether you realise it or not.

When you speak to your partner or children about what to have for tea, you might want Spaghetti Bolognese but they want Carbonara. Your aim is to sell them on why you should have your choice for tea. You might say, "I don't want Carbonara. We had that the other week," or "There's no eggs in the house. I'd have to pop to the shop. Let's have Spag Bol as I have all the ingredients." If they say, "Ok then, let's have Spag Bol," you've won the discussion and sold them on it, haven't you? This is "selling". Persuading someone to do something or agree with you is selling.

Similarly, you might be planning a trip to the cinema. You might want to see James Bond, whereas your partner might want to watch *Titanic*. You might focus on the advantages of picking the right film: "I don't want to see *Titanic*. It's sad at the end. I want some action. Everyone else is saying that the James Bond is really good." So you're using social proof and appealing to their emotions. Again, you're using sales techniques. If they say: "Ok, let's go to James Bond," you've closed the sale.

It's the same all through your life with everything you do each day. People don't think they're in sales. But everybody is in sales.

Truth is: you are already in sales.

You are selling all day, every day, whether you realise it or not.

In every single business, there will be sales or selling. It's the biggest part of the business as this is what brings in all the money. So you need to get your head around the fact that having your own business is going to involve some sales and selling.

You might have to sell yourself as owner of your business. You might have to sell your proposition and how good you are at what you do and your vision to get investors to start it up. You might have to sell yourself to a manufacturer to make your product as cheaply as possible. You might have to sell yourself to a PR firm so that you can promote your product. It is all about selling.

Salespeople have a bad image because of some car salesmen and double-glazing salesmen. We tend to think of dodgy salesmen with pinstripe suits and coffee breath; that they'll rip you off, make false promises and they're just after your money. This is the stereotype that most people think of. As a result, they tend to look down on sales and not want to be associated with it.

Obviously, this might be the case for some of salespeople, but not all of them are like that. If they were, then most businesses wouldn't last five minutes. Think about it: without sales, you will have no business as no money will be coming in. Without sales, it's game over!

SCARED OF SELLING?

Often, people are scared of selling. However, when you dig deeper, the thing that they are scared of isn't selling the product or service. What they are scared of is rejection. They're worried about getting a "no" and then feeling down and low.

Let's be honest, nobody likes rejection. But successful people at the top have probably had more rejection than anybody else. They've just learned not to let it bother them.

Colonel Sanders, founder of Kentucky Fried Chicken, knocked on over a thousand doors with his chicken recipe before someone finally said, "Yes, you can put it in one of my stores." He then went on to build a global empire at the age of 65. Imagine if he'd stopped knocking when he got to his one-thousandth rejection!

There's another lesson here in that people often think you can only set up a business when you're young. There are countless people who've set up a business in their 40s, 50s, and even 60s, and became hugely successful – so age doesn't matter and shouldn't hold you back.

Going back to the idea of rejection, you can never ever get rid of rejection fully. Never. It doesn't matter who you are: Jeff Bezos, Elon Musk, Mark Zuckerberg. They all get rejection, but it's how you deal with it that matters most.

Of course, there are some types of rejection that are really hard to deal with. If it's a life-changing deal for your business or the property deal of a lifetime where you pay all your fees, get your mortgage sorted, and at the last minute the other side pulls out, it's hard to deal with and it's always going to be a blow. But you just have to brush it off.

You might read this and think, *Oh, I just can't handle rejection, so I'm not even going to try.* No one actually likes dealing with rejection. But what we say in sales is, "Every 'no' gets you one step closer to a 'yes'." When you reframe it and flip it on its head like that, it takes some of the harshness away. You think, *Hey, you know what: I'm one step closer to where I want to be now because I've narrowed my search down* – whether that's looking for investors or finding people to buy your products and services.

To use a personal analogy: if you want to have a relationship and find a partner, the more people you speak to, the more chance you've got of finding the right one. It's the same thing essentially: it's a numbers game. Imagine if the first time you ever got rejected by a girl or a guy, you said, "Alright, I'm giving up. I'll never find a partner now. I'm going to be alone forever." No, you wouldn't. Why? Because you know that you'll eventually find someone if you keep asking.

It's the same with any business. Why would you give up on sales just because you've had a few rejections? If you keep going, you'll eventually get the business, the customer, the investment, etc.

Sales is a big part of everything in life. Even if you decide to go to the gym, you've got to sell it to yourself that you should be getting gym membership; that you can do more reps; that you can do an extra 10 minutes on the treadmill. If you didn't sell that to yourself, you would just stop going. You're 'selling' every day in every part of your life.

When you think of it like this, it should take some of the fear away.

If a lion chased a gazelle and couldn't catch it, would it think, *Right, that's it, I cannot catch prey. I'll go hungry forever and die*? I don't think so.

FEAR OF FAILURE

A lot of our fear of failure usually comes from our upbringing. If you're taught that you can't do something a lot when you're growing up, you can do one of two things: you can either believe it or you can choose to prove it wrong.

If you allow yourself to believe it and then instil that as a belief, you will carry that all through your adulthood. It can still be changed, but some people will never get out of that and will always doubt themselves and lack confidence. Then, typically they won't go on to achieve as much if they're always doubting themselves.

The opposite of that is people who use failure or criticism as fuel – like I did – to prove it wrong. They use it as motivation.

We are all products of our environment to a degree. It could have been your schoolteachers, parents, work colleagues or your friends putting you down, saying you're terrible at something. If you're no good at sports and everyone mocks you because you're the worst at football, you'll think that you can't play. A lot of our beliefs are instilled at a young age.

You can't change what happened when you were a child. But you can reframe it and change how you react to it when you're older. You can even use it as rocket fuel!

Make a list of unhelpful messages you had in childhood.

Write a list of their opposites now.

This exercise above will help you change your mindset on what you may have believed or even still believe to this day. Change your limiting beliefs – starting now.

Just because you have been told something about yourself by others doesn't mean it's true. I hear lots of people with a hyena mindset. For example, they might say they can only drive an automatic car as they can't know how to change the gears: "Oh, I couldn't drive a manual car. I couldn't go on the motorways, I'm too scared." That's just a belief. It doesn't mean it's true. But they are programming their minds to believe it.

Similarly, if you think, *I'll never become a millionaire,* guess what you're never going to become? *I'll never have a six pack or be skinny; it's in my genes* – again, guess what's not going to happen? If you think that you're never going to be massively successful in business or have a really beautiful wife or a handsome husband, guess what you're likely to get?

Just because you've never done something before doesn't mean that you're never going to do it in the future. Everybody at the top was once at the bottom. Everybody who's achieved something big was once a baby who didn't know what a business was or what money was. Mark Zuckerberg wasn't born thinking about Facebook when he was wearing a blue nappy. He thought of it at some point later on and believed in himself and made a success of it.

As soon as you realise this, then you get to decide. What do you want your new beliefs to be? What do you want to be true?

What do you want your new beliefs to be?

Make a list right now.

You might decide to think, *I want to be confident*. If you start thinking that you're confident, then you're more likely to start acting in a confident way. You can read up on confident people and speak to confident people. You can watch videos made by confident people and read their books. You can walk, talk, and act like a confident person. It costs nothing to make this shift.

Anybody can start doing this – now today, not tomorrow or next month.

So you just have to start behaving and acting as if you are the person that you want to be. If you want to be the best salesperson, what type of salesperson do you want to be? Imagine all the attributes of the perfect salesperson as if they are in a catalogue. So what are these attributes? Name them.

So your thought process might go something like this:

You would look presentable, because 80 percent of the way that you look, your appearance, is your clothes. You'd be dressed well, in a nice suit or a dress, looking professional. You should be business-like and look the part. You wouldn't look like a scruff, in a tracksuit with a hoodie. You wouldn't have messy hair or a beard that needed trimming. You wouldn't speed onto the driveway of your client's house in a muddy or rusty car with music blasting. You would pull up in a presentable car, either on the drive or pavement beside the house. Then, you would walk slowly up the pavement; not bang-bang-bang on the door, but a firm polite knock. When the door opens, you'd smile. "Hi, it's Terry from Bespoke. Got an appointment at 4 o'clock? Is it Richard? Hey, Richard, how are you doing? Can I come in? Shall I take my shoes off?" Polite, pleasant, good tone of voice. Dress and act the part, and you will win the part.

My point is: think about the ideal person that you want to be. Just think about everything that your ideal role model has and is and does – and then you copy that.

You might want to be the best businessperson in the world. So, think: who is perceived to be the best one? Who do I admire most? What do they do? What are the qualities that I admire? What is their routine? How do they speak to staff? What is their office like? What is their process like?

Make a list of things that you need to do and have and be to become the best version of yourself in every part of your life. Then, go and do it. It's time to let go of any stupid negative hyena beliefs that may have been holding you back for years. Be. A. Lion.

GROWING YOUR BUSINESS

We live in a crazy world now where you can sell stuff on Amazon and become a millionaire. You can do a lot of things even if you have very little or zero money just by using your mind. You could write a book for free and publish it yourself. You can sell your knowledge by creating videos and webinars and online training programmes. You can create online membership sites. Often, it will cost you little apart from your own time. Yet you can still make money from all these things that cost next-to-nothing to set up.

The hyenas will say, "Oh, I haven't got the money to do it, so I can't start up."

So many people look for the reasons why they can't set up a business, more than reasons why they can. The hyenas will say, "Oh, I haven't got the money to do it, so I can't start up."

Well, my answer to that would be: *perhaps do something that doesn't cost any money or go and attract some money from investors.*

To which the sloth might say: "Oh, I don't know anybody that's rich." *So why not write a business plan and go to your bank?* "I don't know how to do one of those." *Then, go online and find out how to write one. Write a business plan and go to investors.* "I don't know any investors …" *Google it!*

Hyenas and sloths will just look for a reason why they can't do something, rather than why they can.

There are so many hyenas and sloths who just aren't proactive enough to do that and they'll just look for a hundred reasons why they can't do something.

If I lost everything tomorrow, I've got no doubt in my mind whatsoever I'd make everything back – and more – because it's the way I think right now and who I am. I just know that I can succeed in whatever I do using the habits and mindset I have now.

Stop telling yourself you can't do something – because 99 times out of 100, whatever you want to achieve, there's somebody else who's already done it. There's always somebody who's worse off than you who has achieved more than you. When you realise that, you understand, *If they can do it I can do it, too.*

RESEARCH YOUR MARKET

Research your market. Look at the competition and what they do. Half the time you'll get inspired by looking at what someone else is doing and you can then put your own spin on it and make it your own. Never copy anything exactly, but I don't think there's anything wrong with copying and improving on an idea. If you think about books on self-development, a lot of them are copied from somebody else. It's difficult to get 100% original content.

There's nothing wrong with looking at other people who are in the space that you want to be in, examining what works for them, and what their strengths are, and then using this as inspiration and making it your own. This is market research.

For example, you might look at your competition and think, *They do this really well, but this part of their service is poor.* You might find a weakness or a hole where you can then insert a strength of your own so you can stand out from them.

If you want to set up a business, look at the big competitors and copy what they do. Don't copy the small start-up in that industry, because you don't know if they're any good or if they're doing well; you don't know if they're going to go bankrupt the following week. You don't want to copy a product or service that doesn't work, you want to copy a successful model! There's no shame in learning from other people.

THERE'S NO SUCH THING AS PERFECT

At the end of the day there's no magic way to set up a business, there's no perfect industry, there's no perfect method. But people think there is. So they watch and they wait. That's why people buy courses. They want the magic ingredient or the special pill that they can take and suddenly they're a millionaire.

That does not exist. The sooner you accept that, the sooner you will realise, *If I'm going to do this, it's up to me. I'm not going to get gifted it. It's not going to be easy. I just have to work my arse off to get to where I want to be and perfect it. I'm going to make mistakes but I've just got to get on with it.*

I think too many people are stalling on chasing the dream and the passion because they think, *But I need to know everything about this industry before I do it.* Then, before you know it, five years has passed and you feel like it's too late.

You've got to sometimes just bite the bullet or jump in at the deep end and that's how you learn how to swim. Forget about the armbands or wanting a life jacket. Forget about worrying if there are any sharks in the water. Just jump in and swim!

Yes, some people will struggle to swim and then they will quit and go back to employed land. They'll forever and a day tell everyone, "I tried starting a business but it was too hard. It's not for me." They'll justify themselves. They'll shout from the rooftops why it didn't work, when in reality if they had just kept moving their arms and legs over a good space of time, then eventually they would have learned to swim. They would have got to where they wanted to go.

TEAM WORK: YOUR PRIDE OF LIONS

Lions are stronger working as a pride than when they are alone.

You cannot achieve the highest highs without a team. The second you think that 'you' are the business, you don't have a business – because you can't do it all yourself.

One simple concept about this is: a business is a commercial and profitable enterprise that runs and grows without you. However, it can't run and grow without a team. If it's just you, then it's a job not a business. You have a high-stress, sometimes high-paid, job!

If you're just a self-employed one-man band—the builder, the dentist, the accountant—it might fit your lifestyle to work alone. That is fine, as not everyone needs a huge, massive team. But this is clearly not a business. You just have a job because your 'business' can't run and grow without you being there.

Even if you have a team of staff, you may not have a good business by this definition. Some people think, *I'm the boss: I'm the most important person in this business. Without me it's all gone. The ship sinks if I'm not here.* I've heard people say that almost proudly. That's not a good thing.

You need to put the right players in the right positions and build your team. If you put a goalkeeper up front, he's probably not going to score very many goals. If you put a midfielder or a little 5 foot 5 fast winger in goal, he's probably not going to save any shots. You need to have the right people in the right positions in order to win the game. If you've got all the right people in the right positions, you might win by 10 goals to 0. If you've got 5 of the 11 players in the right positions, you might draw or win 2-0. If everyone is in the wrong position, you're absolutely stuffed. You're likely to lose 10-0.

If you've got one negative hyena, this can spread to other members of the team and damage your organisation.

Having the right people in the right positions is massive. If you've got one hyena, one person who's negative, this can spread to other members of the team and damage your organisation. It can end up with other staff leaving, you losing income and revenue, and even having your business folding. You could lose everything that you've worked for just by having the wrong people in the wrong positions. That's how important it is.

It's really essential for keeping your business intact and running; it's also really important for growth. You need amazing people who are better than you, because as the boss you can't be the administrator, the salesperson, the leader, the marketer, the bookkeeper, the manager, the sales director, the sales trainer, the operations manager. You can't be all of these people at once. You might have certain skills that you're highly skilled at, but you can't do everything. The answer is to hire the best people in all the other positions, so you've got a full squad of excellent people.

Some people say, "Oh, you need all-rounders." An all-rounder is someone who can do everything: admin, managing, sales, social media, balancing the books, marketing, etc. I don't agree with that. If you try to do too many things, and wear too many hats, it dilutes your impact. In my opinion you're far better having somebody who's a specialist – who's unbelievable at marketing, for example – and putting them in the marketing position and not letting them do any sales or admin; then getting someone who's unbelievable at admin or sales and not letting them do anything else.

Going back to that animal analogy: if you've got some sloths who just plod, who don't move very fast and rely on others to carry them in order to speed up, you may need to get rid of them.

You may need to get rid of sloths who just plod and rely on others to carry them.

If some of your staff are acting like hyenas, then they may need to be gone as well. They have no loyalties, hyenas, as they like to snatch from other people's feasts. They are sly and untrustworthy. They may sound like they're laughing but, in reality, they may be getting ready to attack other team members.

Hyenas have no loyalties. They are sly and untrustworthy.

If you've got a pride of lions around you, then you have a much better chance of success. You can stomp through the savannah hunting together and there's much less chance of your food getting away. You no longer have to do things on your own, so you can save your energies for the things that matter. You can dominate your territory. When you roar collectively as a pride, the sound is heard for miles around.

When you roar with a pride of lions, the sound is heard for miles about.

INTERVIEWING: FINDING YOUR PRIDE

To recruit your first member of staff is interesting when you have a new business. When you advertise for the position, they're going to be your first team member. So you're going to have to sell yourself to that person, as much as they are going to sell themselves to you.

Your first employed person is likely to be an administrator to do all of your paperwork – it was with me. You have to really get that person to believe in you and what you're trying to achieve. You also need to understand what they want and help them achieve it – which is usually earning some money and enjoying their work.

In the interview stage, you need to find people who you want to work with. They've got to be good at what they do, obviously, but you've also got to get along with them. Don't just take someone on because they're your friend or a family member, because a lot of the time that ends in disaster. They've got to be what you're looking for.

Before an interview, if I want to take on somebody for a new role, I will write down what this person needs to be. If I'm hiring a marketer, I write down what a perfect marketer looks like. Then, I try to get someone as close to that description as possible. You might never find *the* perfect person, but if they're 80 percent there, you can get the next 20 percent by coaching and training them.

Initially, when you don't have too much experience, I feel most people should just look for someone they can get along with, because you've got to be able to gel with that person. A lot of it is gut feeling. You have this feeling, don't you, when you meet someone for the first time. I believe that we all have a sixth sense. I believe everybody does; some people more than others. A lot of the time this sixth sense is right. Learn with time to then use your gut and your head. If you master recruitment, you have mastered one of the most important and difficult parts of business.

My mum, who now works for me, is a great example. When someone new comes into my office, I always ask her after the meeting, "What do you think of so and so?" My mum will make her mind up within 10 minutes of meeting a person and she's right most of the time. She seems to have a sixth sense regarding: is this a good person or are they a bit sketchy? Are they a lion worthy of joining my pride or are they a hyena or a sloth?

I've found that women are typically more intuitive, so I'll lean on my team members and ask, "What do you think of this person?" or "What do you think of that person?" If key people who I trust don't trust somebody, then I won't trust them either.

Sometimes you may get it wrong with your gut feeling, but most of the time you'll be right. You need someone who will work well with you and your colleagues in the department they're going to be working in.

Other things to think about are things like eye contact and how they carry themselves. Do they dress like a scruff or take pride in their appearance? If they take pride in how they look, then they normally take pride in their work.

Ask them personal questions as well. It's important for us at Bespoke Financial to employ people who have family values, because we typically help families with life insurance. We tend to help couples with children and a mortgage with insurance, to make sure that if something happens to them – if, heaven forbid, they die or get cancer – they're going to get some money and their children are going to be okay financially. So a 21-year-old guy who doesn't have a partner, children or a mortgage, probably won't be able to connect with our clients because there's little common ground. At the end of the day, people buy from people they like, people who they trust and people who are similar to them.

So I look for nice people with family values. They've got to have integrity. They've got to be honest and trustworthy. No ego—the second you let a big ego into an office, it rocks the boat straight away. We don't want selfish people because they have to work as part of a team. It's important that you have nice people around you and a pleasant working environment.

Once you have your team, treat them well. For example, I give all my staff their birthday off, paid, every year. I treat them well, buy them dinner, and we do team-building exercises. We go for food and drinks together regularly.

Richard Branson famously said something along the lines of: Train your team members to be good enough to leave you, but treat them so well that they never will. That's something that all lions try to do. I train my staff to be the very best and make them elite at what they do. Then, I'll treat them well and make them feel part of something bigger and part of the company mission. We have a common goal to be the biggest and best in the UK. So they are emotionally invested in that goal and want to work here because they get plenty of rewards. They're good enough to leave and set up by themselves, but they stay because it's a nice environment and they want to be part of an award-winning team.

Some people think team building is about going out to have a few pints once a week or a meal at Christmas. They put on daft party hats and pull some crackers and think, *Oh, that's team building. Yeah, I've done that now. Tick. Now they'll stay with us all next year, because they want to work here.*

Really, is that enough? Do you really feel part of something when you have a Christmas do? I don't think so. It needs to be constant and a way of life. You have a role of being a friend, a boss, a mentor, the person they can lean on and get advice from personally as well as in business. It's being everything at once.

Managing people and running a team is the hardest part of our business by a mile and it's the bit that so many people get wrong. So many people have fantastic ideas and business models, but they get it wrong when it comes to their team because they don't know how to manage people.

There are different challenges with managing 50, 100, 1000 people. I met somebody in London recently who manages 20,000 people in an American firm. I thought, *How on earth do they even do it?*

It goes back to my shit stick analogy again. If you want small results and a small bit of shit, have a small team. You're not going to get that many issues with two or three people: maybe the odd sick day; maybe one person has to have some time off work for whatever reason. There's not too much to deal with there.

But if you've got a team of 20,000 people it's going to be a massive manure farm! There will be people arguing. There will be people leaving or you've got to pay them more. One of them will want a pay rise, so they all will want a pay rise. Next thing you know, they're threatening to go on strike. There's just so much shit that comes with having a bigger team of staff. But then, on the other side of that shit farm, there's a bigger business that will generally make more money than the one with three people – for obvious reasons.

Team culture is a huge thing. If you have an award-winning business that's the biggest in the country, you're more likely to believe that you're elite and a winner if you are part of something like that. The culture is then all about winners and winning and thinking big. This will then be very visible in sales, because you have leader boards. For example, we publish leader boards daily about what everybody's done, so there's no hiding and no bullshitting. You can't escape it.

So if you want to be part of this team, you are accountable every day. If someone hasn't sold for a couple of days, they start to feel bad. What does that make them do? It makes them sell every day and step up. Or they feel like they're in the wrong environment, so they go and play for a different team who aren't winning trophies.

If you want to be a lion, you have to act like a lion so that you win at everything.

If you want to be a lion, you have to act like a lion so that you win at everything.

SYSTEMS

In my business, it was just me selling life insurance for ages. Although we were achieving huge things nationally, I was still doing a lot of the selling. Then, as the business started to grow, other people came in and started to sell too.

But it wasn't a proper business until I stepped back and focused on working on my business – and growing my business – rather than working in my business. There is a big difference.

I've already mentioned that the definition of a business is: "a commercial and profitable enterprise that runs and grows without you" as defined by Brad Sugars, the business coach. But this is such an important concept that it's worth mentioning again. So, the self-employed dentist is still self-employed even if he's the director. He's not a business owner if he's looking at teeth as he's still exchanging his time for money. It only becomes a business when that dentist employs another dentist or dental technician to look at people's teeth so that business runs and grows without the owner. He then steps back out of the business and it can operate even without him.

How do you step back from your business so that you're no longer involved on the frontline? You do that by designing systems and processes and manuals that explain every single part of your business about how everything runs.

Imagine if one of your staff leaves. If you have a manual, you can recruit somebody off the street who slots into that position and reads the instructions and processes, so they know what to do without you telling them. That's quite a big task for a lot of businesses, but I believe you don't really have a business until you've got that.

So I did this with the help of my team to design the manuals, systems, and processes that enable my businesses to run and grow without me. Obviously, I'm still going to be in the business to a degree, but I could take a step back for three months and it would still run and grow.

That's a really important message to change people's mindset where they might have a great business where they're making millions of pounds, but if you remove the director—and this happens in most cases—the wheels stop turning, slow down or eventually come grinding to a stop. This is because that person runs everything, oversees everything, tells everyone what to do, gives the orders, and brings in the most amount of revenue.

You need to learn to step back, put your trust in other people, and design systems and processes so that your business runs and grows without you.

I have set up multiple businesses in my career, so when I set up my next one the systems and processes will be done from the get-go, not five years in. Therefore it will be scalable (and sellable) a lot quicker.

AVOID COMPLACENCY

By no means let yourself become complacent. I am recruiting all the time constantly because I want to have a world class team. Even though we're the biggest life insurance business in the UK by quite a way, I'm still pushing, I still want to get bigger.

We actually broke the national record last month by doing 1,340 life insurance policies in one month – which is a UK national record as far as I know. But then we said, "Next March we'll beat that." We did £30,000 in monthly premiums, which has never been done before in the network either. So now we're saying, "How do we get to £50,000?" That compares with Number 2 in the rankings, the next business down from us, which achieved just £12,500 in monthly premiums. So even though we're well ahead already, we're still setting bigger and bigger goals.

A lion mentality is: We're dominating this and we're never ever going to stop.

That's a lion's mentality: *We're dominating this and we're never ever going to stop.* I quite like it when other people come up to me and say, "How do you do it? What are you doing? I don't understand."

I love that because then they almost commit to defeat. It's a bit like the gazelle when it's in the grasslands and he spots a lion coming towards him. He starts to walk backwards to get away. He turns around and there's another lion behind him. Then, he starts to walk to the side … but discovers there's another one there. He walks to the other side … and there's another one there. So there's one in every direction. Then, what will he do? He'll probably just lie down and get eaten! Do that with your competition: be so good that they admit defeat and surrender.

There's no way I could achieve 1,340 policies in one month by myself. It's impossible without sales staff, a sales trainer, and an amazing admin team that submit all the cases and put it all on the computer. It's impossible without an office manager managing those people. It's impossible to have a quality business without a customer care manager who rings all the clients and makes sure they're happy. "Have you had your welcome pack in the post? Were you happy with the service? Were you happy with the advice?" It's impossible to keep up our high quality of service without them.

You can't achieve great things without the right team. There are companies that have more staff than us, but aren't doing half what we do. It's because we have the right people in the right positions.

"You can't achieve big things without the right team."

It's not about having a great CV. I take on people who've never done sales before sometimes, because they're a fresh slate. If you take on salespeople who've done this job before, they've often got bad habits. They'll say: "I used to do it this way," or "I used to do it that way," or "This is what I used to do at my old place." I like to take on people who've never done the job before so I can train them the way I like. I've got this amazing team that is *the* best in the country as a result.

When I interview people, I put a lot of weighting on personal qualities rather than skills. I can teach someone skills, but I can't teach them how to deal with rejection. I can't teach them how to have a personality. I can't teach them how to be funny. I can't teach them how to have good morals; how to do the right thing and have integrity. You've either got these qualities or you haven't.

I can encourage them and help those skills develop with training. But if they haven't got them in the first place, it's pointless. Even if they know life insurance inside out and back to front, even if they're intelligent with years of experience, then that's irrelevant if they've got no personality. This is because people buy people.

People buy off people who they like and trust. The scenario I use with my sales staff is: if you arranged an appointment and someone turned up on your doorstep, you would warm to them instantly if they were nicely dressed and smart.

But if a Goth turned up to your door, with black earrings, hoops in their nose, piercings all over their face, badly clothed with chains on and a Slipknot tee-shirt, with black nail varnish, unfortunately, you judge that person instantly. Even if the Goth is unbelievably good at their job, knows everything about life insurance, and is the best salesperson in the world, he will have to work harder for the sale than the smartly dressed person.

People tend to buy off people who are the same as them – that's a massive driver – so you've got to know your audience and customer.

As well as that, my team are similar to me. A lot of them have children. They also like going out, socialising and having holidays. If you drill down, a lot of their values are the same as mine. I want to do well financially, but I wouldn't compromise my integrity or my family just to make money. None of my team would do that either. They're very similar to me in a lot of ways, because you attract people who are like you.

MANAGING STAFF

The transition from your job to becoming a "boss" can be a steep learning curve. A lot of people who are in sales have the perception that they can run or manage a sales team. However, managing people – especially when you are paying their wages and relying on them to bring in income for your business – is a completely different skill.

When I first started, I thought: *Let's read some books on how to manage people.* I had to relearn how you treat people because it's different when you're an employer.

Ruling with an iron fist like they used to do in the 1980s and 1990s doesn't work anymore. The world is too sensitive and people are too educated. In three clicks of a button, they can find out what their rights are and you can get sued for so many different things. A heavy-handed approach doesn't work anymore: so you've got to guide and encourage people; be the friend but not too friendly, be harsh but not too harsh. You've got to be someone who they look up to. You've got to be someone who is a friend, a mentor, a coach – all those things rolled into one.

The environment I'm in is self-employed insurance sales and I don't give anybody leads. So I have to train people to be good enough to find their own leads, in addition to understanding the 100-odd different products that we've got. So they have to be trained on: product knowledge; how to sell; how not to sell; how to get referrals; how to be self-employed.

It's a tough environment. So you have to separate the lions out from the sloths!

TEAM CULTURE: INCENTIVES AND REWARDS

I think some bosses get this wrong because they have old-fashioned ideas. They think, *My team should do what I want because I'm the boss and I'm paying the wages.* They think everyone should just do as they say.

But the way to get someone to do something is make them want to do it, not to tell them to do it. I could say to my staff today, "You've all got to sell more. This isn't good enough. I'm not happy. You need to work harder." But threats never work as they just annoy people.

It's much better to incentivise people instead: "If you do more of XYZ, you will get ABC." That ABC needs to be something special that they really want, and that makes them want to do it.

So incentives and rewards are key. Different people are driven by different things, so this can't be purely financial. Some people are driven by money, but others are more motivated by recognition. It all just depends on what motivates them.

Incentives are important because you've got to make people want to do something. You can't just demand or expect them to do an amazing job. In my environment, you need to dangle some sort of carrot – such as money, recognition, a spa day, a car.

DEALING WITH HYENAS

If you've ever worked in an office environment, you'll know there's always somebody in the office who's unpleasant. There's always office politics: "Oh, he's horrible," or "She's bitchy," or "She always talks behind your back." I've had one person who I had to get rid of like that.

As a general rule, aim to have an office that is peaceful or full of laughs. In our offices, everyone's laughing, smiling, joking most of the time, but also doing their work. It's a lovely environment because I'm careful not to hire hyenas.

Hyenas are not to be trusted. Not ever. They may sound like they are laughing. But often that eerie giggle means they are about to attack their prey.

Hyenas may sound like they're laughing. But that eerie giggle often means they are about to attack their prey.

If you have team members who are causing huge headaches, negatively impacting on a lot of other people, and causing you issues, then ideally you need to encourage them to move on.

We live in a world where you can't just get rid of somebody or sack them. You've got to follow a process: a verbal warning, written warning, and follow HR process. So you can't sack them on the spot, even if you want to.

In order for me to get rid of somebody, they would have to do negative things quite a few times, because I do believe that people make mistakes and human errors do happen.

Let's say they make a mistake on a document, it's human error. But if it's a personality issue such as this person has upset someone else, shouted at them or become aggressive, for me that's less acceptable.

Obviously, if someone's bad at their job and they keep making mistake after mistake after mistake, then you need to take the appropriate action. But when someone is nasty or horrible to somebody else, I think that's when you have to act quicker, because that impacts on others.

BURN-OUT

I think everybody has down days – days where you have less energy than others. Everyone has had the days where you wake up and think, *Oh, I can't be bothered to do it.* I have them too.

Loads of people in my office say, "Why have you got loads of energy, Terry?" as I get up at 5am every day. But I still have bad days, too. I just don't show it or other people don't see I've had a bad day because I don't let myself show it.

My morning routine gets me away from any negative talk, because I'll exercise, and do some reading and goal setting which gets me in the right frame of mind.

I think the people who talk about burnout are typically doing things that they don't enjoy or are unhappy in some way or another. If you're doing well in all parts of your life and you're passionate about what you're doing, working 12–15 hours may make you tired, but I don't think you'll crash.

There's a belief that if you work too much, you'll always get burnout. But I'm not sure that's true. At the very start of my business, I worked 14-hour days seven days a week. I put everything into it.

But if you love what you're doing, it doesn't feel like work. In fact, it's a good feeling when you're making progress and you're doing things you're passionate about.

If you feel like that every day, how on earth can you possibly get burnt out? In fact, you want more of it, because you're doing that you love.

DISTRACTIONS

About two years ago, I did a detailed analysis of how I was spending all my time. For 2 weeks, I kept a diary with 15-minute blocks from when I woke up to when I went to sleep. This is a really eye-opening exercise and I would highly recommend it. I discovered from this that I was spending around 3 hours on emails a day.

Not only this, but I was allowing emails to interrupt my other tasks. When an email popped up, when I was in the middle of a task, it was disturbing me. It was distracting me from what I was doing and making me late for my next meeting.

So I literally thought, *What on earth am I doing? This needs to stop.*

I then decided to turn off all my email notifications on my phone so I don't get the ping-ping-ping all the time. I turned off the notifications on my desktop and my laptop, so it didn't ping there either. When I started doing this, it was a revolution.

You can even put a bounce-back message on your emails that says, *Hi. Thank you for emailing me. I only check my emails once a day. If it's urgent, please call me on this number below. The reason why I do this is to be ultra-productive and run all the businesses that I run. Thank you.*

I recommend that you do the same to increase your own productivity. Half the time, emails can wait; they don't have to be dealt with there and then. If it's urgent, people will ring you.

This was a big thing for me that enabled me to be really efficient and achieve more. It's about controlling your own time rather than getting distracted or letting other people dictate how you spend your time.

GROWING YOUR BUSINESS AT THE RIGHT SPEED

Once you have a good team around you, you can start to grow your business.

It's going to be slow at the start, obviously. You don't want to take on 20 people all at once, because that's hard to manage, especially if you have limited experience and you're learning as you go.

You've also got to have systems and procedures in place in order to scale up your business. This means creating "How-to" Files for your office, which I touched upon briefly, earlier.

The How-to Files are for the administrators if they ever ask a question, such as: "How do you put this onto the CRM?" This streamlines the process considerably, as the reply becomes so standard that everyone knows it: "Have you looked in the How-to Files?"

So I try to create a culture where people find the answers out for themselves. Better still: if they ask about something that's not in the How-to Files, when they find out the answer, they are then asked to write it up and put it in the How-to Files.

So, eventually, they don't need to keep asking people, "What about this?" and "What about that?" The habit is to first go to the How-to Files. This is then a system that has all the answers on how to run your business.

So, you need to systemise every single part of your business in the same way. For example, I've systemised the sales process for Bespoke. We've got the Bespoke Bible, which explains every aspect of how to sell, how to close, how to get referrals. I give this guide to anybody new coming into this business.

This gives them all the answers to questions such as:

- How do I close sales?
- How should I conduct myself in appointments?
- How should I dress?
- How do I send a case to admin?
- How do I get referrals?

Every question they might be likely to have is answered there. If it's not, then it soon gets added.

In this way, everything gets systemised. Create How-to Files for your team and also a "bible" that has absolutely everything in, so someone else can run things for you if needed them to.

Remember: the definition of a business is a commercial and profitable enterprise that runs and grows without you. If you are solely relying on a sales director to train your sales staff, what happens if they get sick, are off work, go on holiday or leave?

If you haven't got a How-to Manual and a system for someone else to come in and say, "There's the manual. That's how you do our training. Crack on!" that's not a business, because it crumbles as soon as one person's off. It's absolutely imperative for growth to have systems and processes in place if you want to grow your business.

Another analogy would be that you have to get the foundations right in order to build a tall building. What happens if you're building a hundred flats in a tower and the foundations aren't structurally sound? If you've got weak foundations and it's only one storey high, it's probably not going to fall down. But as you grow, the foundations become increasingly important. The higher it goes, the more chance it has of falling down. Strong foundations mean: having the right people in the right positions; and having a system and process so that everything is documented in a How-to Manual.

I suspect that this is why you see a lot of family businesses that get passed on to younger generations going bankrupt. They go bust because the kids don't know what they're doing. They often don't have manuals or systems and processes to slot into. They're not used to dealing with large sums of money, so they end up spending it all. Or there are members of the team who leave because they liked working for the dad, but they don't like the arrogant son who thinks he knows everything and he's shouting at everybody. That son who came in isn't the right player for the position, then the negativity spreads, and the combination of all these things ends up with the business folding.

If you have processes and systems in place, you can be reasonably confident that if you leave your business for six months, when you come back it will be bigger and better.

I'm confident that my business would run and grow without me, because I've intentionally set it up that way. At the start, seven and a half years ago, I went about it in the wrong way. I thought *I'm the main man. I'm running this ship. I'm the best at life insurance in the country.*

I didn't have any skills in management, because when you start you don't. I took on an administrator first, then I took on some salespeople, and then it just grew and grew and grew. Gradually, you learn the skills you need and you build up the systems and processes so that it can run without you.

I was then able to go on to set up multiple businesses.

GROWTH AND GOAL SETTING

Continual growth is essential, because the second you start to think, *We've made it! We're the best at this*, you get complacent.

The moment you get complacent, even if you're the Number 1 business in your industry, you'll find that Number 2 is snapping at your heels. Number 2 may even be trying everything they can to poach your clients and customers to get ahead of you.

Therefore, if you just stopped evolving and growing and developing, someone else would soon be trying to surpass you.

So you have to have a mindset where you never stop growing; you're constantly trying to get to the next level and setting yourself new goals in every part of your business.

There's no end to it. It shouldn't be a matter of, *Once I get my business to this size I'm done.*

You may have a goal to grow your business so that you can sell it. Personally, if I'm doing something that I enjoy, making good money for me and my family, working with people I like, in an industry I'm passionate about, why on earth would I want that to stop?

Why would I say, "When I get there, then I'm done?" I get a lot of fulfilment just from growing, from achieving new things, and breaking new ground.

IS SCALING UP RIGHT FOR YOU?

Scaling up isn't for everybody. You can still have a very successful and profitable business that isn't huge.

But if you want to achieve something massive, make your mark in history or if you want to become a household name nationally or internationally, you have to scale up.

Having 10 staff and having 100 staff is very different. Having 100 staff and having 1000 staff is very different again. It moves up in levels.

You need key team members around you, each with a strong skillset. They need to have different skills to yours. You don't want too many people who are similar to you or with the same skills as you, because then you're likely to be thinking in similar ways and you're never going to be see the other side of the coin.

Avoid having yes-men or yes-women around you. You need people with different characteristics and skillsets that cover all the bases—someone who's good with numbers, someone who's good with PR, someone who's good with intellectual property, someone who's good with logistics, whatever it may be.

You can't be a huge company without scaling up. You can't make millions and millions of pounds a year. You have to scale up to reach that next level.

HAVING A LIFESTYLE BUSINESS VS SELLING UP

Selling a business eventually is the end goal for a lot of people. That's why they build their business – in order to sell it and get a six- or seven-figure cheque. Selling a business and exiting their business is their idea of utopia.

But you can also choose to have a lifestyle business. This is a business that's really successful and gives you such a great lifestyle that you may never want to sell it. If the business runs and grows without you, you don't have to get too involved, you're making great money and working with great people, why would you want to sell up?

There is no hard and fast rule that says you must eventually sell up and exit your business. You don't have to. So, this is something you need to weigh up.

In your mid-20s, would you want to sell your business for millions and then stop working? I suspect that most people in their 20s wouldn't want to do this. Whereas when you're in your 60s, your view may be quite different.

Get advice: speak to people who've already sold their own businesses before you decide to sell yours. Make sure that it's the right thing for you to do and consider if you'd get the right amount of money for it.

Some people sell their business, then get really down and depressed. If someone's worked in a business for 20 years, it's been their life up that point. If they sell it, even if they make millions of pounds, they might end up sitting at home twiddling their thumbs with no sense of purpose. Or they might go on holiday and enjoy it for a month, but they might lose their get up and go, and not know what to do with themselves.

So you've got to think about that as well. If you're going to sell, maybe you should have an idea or a plan of what you're going to do afterwards. Sometimes you'll have a transition period where you still work there for a couple of years, but make sure you know what you're going to do next. You may have plans to travel the world or to help with a charitable cause or perhaps do some public speaking or write a book. You don't want to be sitting in the house with loads of money and nothing to do.

Bear in mind that a business has to be a profitable enterprise that runs without you. So no one's going to buy it if, when they remove you, it doesn't make money any more or it crashes and burns. So it needs to flourish and be profitable even when you aren't there.

Your customers and clients need to be attached to your brand, and not just to you personally.

When a company buys another business, they look for synergies. They won't necessarily want to buy it and keep it the way it is. They're more likely to want to buy it and increase its value by doing X, Y and Z. They'll want it to have synergies with other businesses that they may already own. They've got to be able to add value to it as well when they buy. These are things to bear in mind as you need your business to be as attractive as possible to potential buyers if you are planning to sell it.

GOAL SETTING

I mentioned earlier in this book that my business broke a sales record for monthly premiums in October 2021. We had just achieved something that has never been done before, but we were immediately thinking: *What next?*

If you don't set that next thing, you stagnate. There's no growth and no challenge. There's nothing to get you up in the morning. So we're already putting plans in place to increase our monthly goal.

This requires a whole new level of thinking. Because if we think the way we've always thought, we'll never get there. The way we think right now got us to £30,000 premiums per month. So we need to think and act differently to get to £50,000. So our new challenge is: How do we do that? We've got nobody to ask because nobody else has done it.

So we need to stretch ourselves and think, *How do we actually do it?* So a simple answer is: we need more people. We know an average of how much each salesperson brings in. Therefore, we need to increase the sales force by X amount to get that, working off an average of what they bring in.

Sometimes people complicate a business when it doesn't need to be complicated if you use the fundamentals, key principles and just basic numbers.

THE POWER OF SIMPLICITY

Not every industry is simple. However, there are simple fundamentals that apply to all businesses. Sales and marketing is a fundamental in every business, regardless of what it is.

Then, there are loads of things that come with that like the price point and profit. In addition, you've got to have a product or a service that has got to be the best it can be.

You've got to market and sell your product or service. How are you going to sell it and how are you going to make any money if you're not marketing it?

Even if your product is the best in the world, if nobody knows about it then nobody's going to buy it.

A lion's life is simple: sleep, eat and reproduce. There's not much more to it. It does all three of them very well to my knowledge (well, certainly the eating part – I don't pay too much attention to the other two parts!) Make your business simple with key actions and it should thrive.

PRODUCTIVITY AND TIME MANAGEMENT

The business guru and author, Brian Tracy, has some really sound advice on time management. He calls it the ABCDE method:

A tasks – are the most important tasks which have consequences if you don't do them.

B tasks – are important but don't have huge consequences if you don't do them.

C tasks – are not really that important, and don't really have consequences either, but they still have to be done.

D tasks – can be delegated

E tasks – can be eliminated.

If you look at the concept of "work", it's about directing your energies to what is most useful to you in achieving your goals (whether that's money, relationships, health or something else). However, it's easy to get caught up doing admin or social media posts or other activities that take you away from your goals. Often, people get distracted and do the wrong things first.

Sometimes on your to-do list you'll have something that is pretty pointless or which you could give to somebody else, but you end up doing it anyway because it seems easier to do it yourself. People typically do the easy things first. But whether something is hard or easy, you should do the most important things that help you achieve your goals first.

That's how I prioritise what I do every day. I work solely on one task until it's done, so I won't get distracted. It's just about planning every single day and prioritising what I'm doing. I then aim to have tunnel vision on one task until it's done. That can't happen if you're getting emails pinging mid-task or if you get distracted and end up doing something else. It's about staying focused on that one task until it's done before then moving on to the next task. It's a great feeling when you scrub something off your to-do list. It gives a sense of achievement and accomplishment.

So, to-do lists are massively important and you're definitely more productive by having a list. But equally important is splitting that list into priorities and working on one separate task at a time until it's done. This will make you ultra-productive compared to someone who just goes with the flow and has so much to do that they end up missing or forgetting things.

In life, especially when you're running a business, nobody gives you instructions. If you're employed and have a job role, you get told what to do by your boss. But if you don't have a boss, there's nobody to prompt or guide you. So, it can be easy to end up doing the wrong things or faffing about doing things that don't get you any closer to your goals.

You have to design your own to-do list every day so that it gives you clear instructions and keeps you on track.

EAT THAT FROG

Another useful tip that Brian Tracy gives is in his book *Eat that Frog!*

The 'frog' he's referring here is the task you don't want to do each day. There's an old saying that if the first thing you do each morning is eat a live frog, then you'll have the satisfaction of knowing it's the worst thing you'll have to do all day.

Your 'frog' is your most challenging task and the thing you're most likely to avoid and procrastinate on. But if you get it out of the way, you'll get everything else done a lot faster.

So, rather than having an unwanted 'frog' hanging around you, causing negative energy, he recommends that you tackle it straight away. If you do it early on, you'll find it so much easier to nail the rest of your to-do list each day.

YOU CAN DO IT

You're never going to get anywhere unless you try. You're always going to be stuck in the same place. So, sometimes you have to take a leap of faith. You have to jump in at the deep end. You have to just go for it even though it might feel daunting.

If you are happy with where you are right now, that's fine, of course.

But ask yourself: would you want to get to the last day of my life and think, *I wish I left that job. I wish I did something I enjoyed. I wish set up that business. I wish I made a go of it.*

Business might not be for you. But you won't know unless you give it your best shot. It's definitely not for you if you don't try! And you'll never find out.

So, you have literally two options: you either do it or you don't.

If you don't, you've got to resign yourself to being in the same place you've always been.

If you do it, then you've got a fantastic opportunity to achieve your dreams. However, you've got to really go for it and put your heart and soul into it. If you follow the fundamentals and the key principles and you work hard, you should get to where you want to be.

My rally cry to you is: you can do it. So just go for it!

BE A LION:
IN PROPERTY

CONNECT WITH ME

Take pictures of your journey as a lion – include photos of yourself; sections of this book that you find helpful; quotes that you like; your list of goals, etc. Then, post it and tag me on Instagram.

THE PROPERTY WILDERNESS

The property wilderness consists of:

Lions

Those who buy 10, 20, 50 properties per year. They do £20 million deals each year, never saying the market is too hot that they can't find deals. There are deals in every market and strategies that work in every market, and they know this, They get shit done no matter what. They feast on their prey every day – no excuses no limits

Hyenas

They say, "Property is risky", "What happens if the boiler breaks?", "What happens if they don't pay their rent?", "What happens if there is a property crash?", "You will lose money in property," "Stocks and shares are better than property; you'll make more money doing them." No matter what you do or how many properties you buy, they have something negative to say.

Sloths

They usually don't own any investment properties; some don't even own a house they live in. They will never have enough money to buy an investment property and don't understand how property even works and never will. Sloths are destined to be average and never change their life or progress.

UNDERSTANDING MONEY

It's important to increase your financial IQ and understand how money actually works. If you've got money in the bank at the moment, you'll get less than 1% interest. But inflation in this country for this year is currently around 5 %. So, if the cost of living is going up by 5 % and you're only getting 1% interest, therefore your money is devaluing by the difference between those 2 rates while it's sitting in a savings account.

Therefore, if you just have cash in the bank, you're losing money! A great phrase from my good friend Danny Inman is "Cash in the bank, is complete wank!" Surprisingly, a lot of people still don't understand this concept. They have been conditioned to think they should save money for a rainy day and keep all their money in the bank because it's safe and it's important to get out of debt as quickly as you can.

However, successful people understand that there is good debt and there is bad debt.

Yes, you should get out of bad debt. But equally important: you need to acquire more good debt, which will help to produce an income for you and your family. There are a great many books that cover this principle, such as Robert Kiyosaki's *Rich Dad Poor Dad,* so I won't go into it in great detail in my own book. However it's essential to understand this basic concept.

People think that they have to just exchange their time for money. They think, *I just have to go to work, put my time into this machine—* their job or their career—and *it spits out some money at the bottom.*

In reality, yes, you have to do that. But once you get to a stage where you've acquired some money, you should ideally invest that money in a vehicle that then produces more money.

Once you do this, the pressure of having to exchange your time for money and having to go to work will reduce with time. Once your assets produce enough income to cover all of your bills, you become financially free.

Many people are just going through life without understanding this; without realising there is a way out of the rat race. There is a way out of exchanging your time for money all of the time until you're 65. There is a legitimate way to do this which is via property investing.

WHY INVEST IN PROPERTY?

I always thought property was a good place to put your money. I liked the idea of getting paid a regular income once I had invested in a property. Once you've bought a property, that then pays you for life. If you structure the finance and the mortgage properly, it will pay you forever. I really liked that idea because I've never had a regular wage. I've always been self-employed since the age of 19, so I liked the idea of creating a regular income for yourself that comes in every month.

In my view, property is *the* best investment you can make. Apart from investing in yourself and your education, there's no other better investment. Property gives you capital appreciation, so your asset will grow in value ... and it gives you positive cash flow every month. There are not many other things that do that.

It's something that's tangible. It's not a stock or a share which is just a number on a computer screen that you can't touch or feel. Property is something you can see and touch. For me, it is just the best investment.

MY FIRST STEP INTO PROPERTY

I first got involved in property investment while I was still working for MetLife, about 10–11 years ago. I remember one day looking online and seeing a house for sale for £15,000. So I went and viewed it. It was a horrible property on a horrible street, with druggies everywhere, but I spoke to the Council and asked, "What would somebody get on benefits?" Then, I asked a lettings agent how much I could rent a house for in that street. I was told £385 a month. I had about £40,000 in my account at the time, so I thought, *Right, I'm going to buy one.*

I knew nothing about property; I had done no courses. I'd watched *Homes Under the Hammer* and that was probably it. I bought my first house with cash, then spoke to the lettings agent and got a tenant in quickly at £385 per month. Four or five months later, the model seemed to be working well, so I thought, *This is great. I'm going to buy another one.* So, I bought another one in the same street, for £16,500. That meant I was getting over £700 a month in profit. Each month, I would think, *Bloody hell, this is good.* I'd still never done a course or watched a video or read a book on property.

So, as the strategy seemed to be working, I bought a third one. I went to an auction to buy one on the next street along. I got outbid but there was another lot that came up and I ended up buying it blind for £17,500. I'd never seen it: just an external picture in the auction catalogue. That should have been a red flag because showing an external picture usually means it's terrible inside. I bought it because I thought, *Nothing will go wrong.*

Anyway, I drove down the street. There was a row of about 30 houses on either side with this one in the middle. Every single house was boarded up, with burnt out cars, rusty swings, fly-tipped trollies and all sorts of crap in the gardens. This one was the only one that wasn't boarded up. There were loads of caravans and dodgy-looking characters at the bottom of this street. My stomach sank as I pulled up. I thought, *What on earth? Oh my god, what have I done? I'm going to probably get murdered or robbed here.*

I locked up my car and went in the house. As soon as I turned the key and opened the door, this smell hit me. I had to pull my jumper over my nose as there was animal shit piled up higher than the skirting boards and a rotten birdcage with mountains of crap in. It was so bad it was burning my eyes. This was in the living room when I walked in.

I got into the kitchen and the sink was rotten with mould. It was horrific. Then I looked out at the back garden and there was a horse tied to the fence. I got back in the car and drove away, thinking, *What have I done? This is just messed up.*

But once I got past the initial shock, I started to think like a lion. Then I started thinking, *Don't worry about it. I'll get some of the lads to come here and strip the place out. Power through the situation: remain calm and positive, act like the lion that you are. I can sort this situation out quickly and efficiently.*

I tried to hire some labourers to clear it out. Waste removal people will take on most jobs and I was offering to pay them over the normal rates to strip the house out. But they were literally turning the job away. Three different people got there and said, "I'm not touching that house. It's too bad. I can't work there."

But eventually I found someone who was willing to do it and managed to get it turned around. I got three tenants in at £385 each, so I was making over £1000 profit per month now after the house of horrors was turned around and rented out. I was thinking, *This is unreal. Even if the properties are disgusting when I buy them, people will rent them after they're done up.*

Then, within the space of about two months mountains of shit hit the fan, I was at the gym one day when I got a call from the police saying that there was an attempted murder in one of my properties. Someone had been stabbed: I was quizzed about the tenants and all sorts. I also had one of my properties broken into, with the door smashed in. I had drug dealers in one, I had the boiler pinched in one. It was just a disaster in all three of them within a short space of time.

I could have just given up at this point. But I didn't. I reassessed the situation and thought, *I need a different strategy: I'm not going to buy really scruffy properties any more. I'm going to buy nicer ones.* I still had never done a course or any training at this point.

So I sold those properties at auction two months after the person got stabbed. I didn't make any money; I literally broke even, pretty much to the pound, just to get them off my hands. I sold them all in an auction in London. After that, I then started to buy properties worth about £80,000 to £100,000, with a 25 percent deposit and 75 percent loan. Then, that gravitated to the BRR (Buy Refurb Rent) strategy. Next, I went into HMOs (Houses of Multiple Occupation), and then serviced accommodation. Now, I'm buying small hotels.

I used to own everything in my personal name. Then, in 2017, I read *Rich Dad, Poor Dad* and I got obsessed with watching motivational videos on business and property. I watched or read *Cashflow Quadrant, Secrets of the Millionaire Mind,* 10x etc as well as books by authors like T. Harv Eker and Grant Cardone. I learned about putting property into limited companies and all of the quirky strategies that you can use, such as using bridging loans. I am still to this day completely obsessed with self-development books and videos. I read or listen to something every day without fail: it is now part of my identity. If you want massive success, I suggest you make this a habit of yours too.

HAVING A NO-LIMIT LIFE

From 2017. I started to ramp things up. In 2019, I bought 16 property units. In 2020, I bought 8 (Covid screwed my plans). In 2021, I bought 13. My goal is to have bought 100 property units by age 35 and 1000 property units by age 45. And I know for sure it is already a done deal unless I change my mind – that is the only thing that will stop me from achieving this.

Going back to what I first said about thinking like a lion and having a no-limit life, I was willing to accept the problems, then dust myself back off and try again. Some people say 10 properties is enough. It might be for some people: 1000 properties might seem too much to achieve. But I honestly do not have a limit; I just don't. I don't think there's any reason why I can't achieve that. I want to be one of the biggest property entrepreneurs in the country. I must give my good friend Tom Smyth credit for the inspiration of my 1000-property goal.

So, I'm planning to carry on doing this side by side with my business. I don't see it as choosing to do one or the other. Just like a lion doesn't have to choose between zebras or wildebeest or gazelles, you can have it all. I honestly believe that. And my message to you is that you can too.

A lion doesn't have to choose between zebras or wildebeest or gazelles. You can have it all.

I don't want to ever go full-time in property. I will always have other business interests because I enjoy it. So I will continue to have multiple businesses in multiple industries in addition to investing in property. In addition, I'll be healthy, I'll have great relationships and I'll have a great life.

THE 4 PS OF PROPERTY INVESTMENT

If you are new to property investment, it may initially seem complicated. But if you break property down into four parts, it is really simple and easy to understand.

Yes, there are loads of different strategies and quirky methods for doing things, and all these extravagant flashy strategies that people talk about online.

However, I like to break it down into the 4 Ps:

1. Property.
2. Paper.

3. People.
4. Price.

1. Property

You've got to make sure it's the right property in the right area at the right price. You've got to make sure it's the right property for your strategy and also that the strategy is right for you.

2. Paper

This is about documents and having the right paperwork.

- Does it need a licence?
- Does it need planning permission?
- What about your finance documents?
- Have you got the right mortgage for it?
- Have you got the right insurance?

Make sure you've got all the correct paperwork for the property.

3. People

You have to get the right type of tenants in your properties. You don't want to be buying a swanky buy-to-let for £2 million and then putting students in it. You need the right type of tenants in your property because you don't want them to damage your investment and devalue it.

4. Price

This is the big P. You've got to buy your property at the right price. You've got to have the right price on the insurance, the finance, the planning, the architects, etc. Then you've got to charge people the right rent as well, because you don't want to be charging too little – but you also don't want to be advertising it for too much because no one will rent it.

Property is quite simple. There's a lot of noise online covering all these complicated strategies and quirky ways of investing in property—no-money-down deals and buying properties for a £1, for example. Sometimes you've just got to decide on one strategy and run with it and perhaps try another strategy after that. Don't try to be too complicated and do too many things at once. Do the basics and simple things first.

Inevitably in life, there will always be hyenas that come snapping at your heels.

BEWARE FALSE PROMISES

You're not going to get rich overnight. Property is not about get rich quick; it's get rich eventually. Far too many property training courses tempt new students with the promise of: "You can leave your job in a month if you come do my course." It's a lie. It's giving people a false sense of security and getting them in financial difficulty by selling them a dream. Yes, the odd person might be able to do this, but the vast majority won't. It's a long-term thing, not get rich quick.

There are loads of 'experts' online hooking people in with the promise of 'replace your income in a week' and all sorts of nonsense.

They're giving people false hope saying, "Leave your job and be full-time in property." Half of them don't even have properties themselves or they have very few. They're telling people to leave their jobs when in reality there's nothing wrong with having a job in addition to buying lots of property. It doesn't have to be an either/or!

Having whatever you want means completely different things to different people. But you don't have to quit your job to be successful in property and you don't have to have a business to buy property either. You can be employed and buy property. You can raise finance or joint venture. You can add so much value to your job that you're given a pay rise and you force your boss to promote you because you're that good at your work. I think that's a much better message to get out than, "Buy my £20,000 course and I'll help you become financially free in seven days."

REAL-LIFE MONOPOLY

I don't invest in property full-time. I use my business to fund a lifestyle to create an income that I can live off and I invest in property to create passive income. I have a business so that I can enjoy myself and earn a good living, but also to buy property. Once you buy enough property, it produces enough income to then buy more property. I don't pay myself anything from my property business currently. The rent just funds more property purchases and continues to. Once you get to a certain level of rent, mine probably funds an extra deposit a month at the moment, so it has a momentum of its own. That's why it's a 'get rich eventually' investment! Because once you've got that momentum and your properties are funding more properties, five years later you'll be remortgaging and pulling out £120,000 here, £30,000 there, or whatever the figures are if you wish to do so.

As an example, with one property recently I've done about £30,000 worth of work on a £200,000 purchase, but I'm now pulling out £120,000, because it went up in value so much. That's tax-free money because it's a loan effectively. What other asset class can you do that with? Not much. I'm not going to just go and spend that on holidays; I'm going to reinvest that. That money has then created an extra 3 to 4 deposits for more properties. So, just time owning that property has created that money.

If my properties all double in value in 20 years, they will create over £5 million worth of equity. If I stop working now and live off the rent (which I'm never going to do), I'll benefit from around £20,000 to £30,0000 a month in rent. During that 20-year period, rent will go up as well.

So why wouldn't you want to start doing that for yourself and your own family? You can if you want to. The only thing stopping you is you. If you tell yourself you're not going to do it or you're not good enough, you're won't be. You've got to just go for it …

I am just as passionate about property as I am about business, because they're both amazing. If I was solely looking at income, the return on investment in business is higher than property. However, I love every part of property investment, not just the returns.

I love finding the deals and negotiating. I love the refurb element of it: seeing a building rundown and then how it is transformed after that. I love working out the numbers at the front end.

Sometimes, I view the property or I'll get someone else to do it for me. I just work out the numbers. What's it worth? What can I offer? I do that negotiation, win the deal and get it secured. I've never even been inside some of the properties I've bought. I've just done the numbers and negotiating at the front end and know it's a good deal. I then pass it to my team to handle. Now, I've got someone who manages the refurb and someone who does the refurbs, companies who manage the let, manage my mortgages and insurance. It's all systems and processes now, built with the intention of scaling and buying in volume as quickly as possible.

When I first started, I knew the full address and postcode of every property. I was on site: I viewed it myself. I've never done the building work myself, but I managed the refurb. I picked the kitchen and bathrooms. I went to the carpet shop and picked the carpets. I chose the colours. I used to do all that and then I used to be there when the estate agent was taking the photos. I used to ring the letting agent to chase them, "Is it let yet? What have you got it on for? How many viewings have we had?"

I don't do any of that any more. I don't know half the addresses I own and I definitely don't know any of the postcodes. I've got them in a spreadsheet. So your role changes over time as your investment portfolio grows. You want to get involved in every part of it at the very start. But once your portfolio starts to grow, that changes.

I love collecting property – it's a little like playing real-life Monopoly. I am a little addicted to buying property. I don't think I could stop even if I wanted to. I got one agreed in the last week: a 12-bed hotel. My goal is to create huge wealth and own hundreds and hundreds, and probably thousands, of properties for me and my family.

What is your goal? What would you like to do for your family and in what timeframe? What is your first step going to be?

> **WHAT IS YOUR GOAL?**
>
> **What would you like to do for your family?**
>
> **What is your timeframe?**
>
> **What is your first step going to be?**

EDUCATING YOURSELF ABOUT PROPERTY

My main tip is to educate yourself first before you get started in property investment. I didn't for the first 3 or 4 years and, as a result, I bought a load of rubbish properties.

The fact that you're reading this book in itself tells me that you're into self-development. When I started investing in property, it wasn't as popular so there wasn't as much content or training out there. Now, there's no excuse. So educate yourself and avoid trying to do a million things at once. Decide on one strategy and do that one strategy first, because it'll give you more clarity of thought. It'll give you a clearer sense of direction and make it easier for you to crack on.

Bear in mind that you can be the best-educated person in the world and know everything about lease options and buy-to-let and HMOs. But if you don't take any action, it's a complete waste of your time. So you need to take action.

There are a lot of people out there who do course after course and spend tens of thousands of pounds on education. But they don't do anything with it, because they get analysis paralysis and take no action.

So educate yourself, then go to work. Sometimes you have to just not think too much – understand the basics, then go and find a property. Start with a buy-to-let. Get your first buy-to-let so that you can get used to: dealing with estate agents; dealing with banks for your finance; dealing with the brokers; dealing with the builders doing the refurb; dealing with the insurance companies insuring it; and dealing with the letting agent when you let it out.

In addition, it will get you used to issues with tenants moving in, tenants moving out, the boiler breaking, the cooker not working. There's always something that needs attending to.

Don't attempt to try something crazy like create a 25-bed HMO for your first investment. A lot of people get that shiny penny syndrome and want to set big goals. But if you make a mistake – which you probably will in the early stages – it's going to be a costly mistake and you don't want to put unnecessary stress or added pressure on yourself. One thing at a time. Remember the saying: how do you eat an elephant? It's one piece at a time. You couldn't try to eat a full elephant in one go. It needs to be tackled bit by bit.

Learn the craft. If you want to become a brain surgeon, it probably means nine years at university just to train. After that, you would still have additional hands-on learning on the job as well. So treat property investment with the same amount of respect. Don't just do 11 years of research and reading. Perfect your knowledge little by little. Buy one property a year for the next couple of years to get used to the process. If you've got loads of money, then your situation is different in where you can start, but still do one thing at a time.

GETTING STARTED WITH LITTLE OR NO MONEY

Check the basics like speaking to a broker to see if you can get a mortgage first.

If you can't get a mortgage because you've got bad credit, there are still things you can do. First, you have to work on your credit score, and secondly, you also need to look at a different way of acquiring property.

Don't believe that you can't invest in property because you have no money, because that's not true. There are still ways to get involved in property even with little or no money.

In 2021, using social media I raised £260,000 of angel finance without really trying too hard or committing too much time to it. These are people who have approached me saying they either don't have the time or they don't have the experience or knowledge to buy property but they've got the money. So these people invest with me for a fixed return. If they invest £100,000 with me, for example, I will give them 8 percent per year. So I will give them £8,000 worth of interest per year, then their full investment back at the end of a one-year or two-year period. This is how angel investing works. This is great for them: it's like getting the benefits of property but without having to deal with mortgages, tenants and estate agents, plus all the things that can go wrong with refurbishing a property.

People lend me money. In return, I give them a personal guarantee that they can make me sell the property (or my businesses) or take legal action against me in the unlikely event that I couldn't pay the money back to them.

There are lots of people out there who will lend you money on an angel investment basis. It might be a friend or a family member initially. If you've got no property and no experience, you're probably not going to get someone from Dubai with a few hundred grand investing in you because they don't know you and you've got no track record. But your friends and family might be able to do that with you when you are first getting started.

I also work with quite a few investors. So if you don't have the time or experience, but you want a steady return on your money, please do contact me on Instagram to talk it through. I'm always happy to work with people who have read my book.

So there are various ways of attracting angel finance. You could do a joint venture with someone who has the money but doesn't have the time to go and source the property and do everything else. Ask yourself: "Who are the people I know who have money?" Can you reach out to them about being an angel or doing a joint venture with them? People with money generally like making money and that's what you are offering them, a way for them to make interest on their savings. It's a win for them just as much as it's a win for you.

Another way of investing in property when you have little money is to buy it using a lease option. This is one of several ways to invest in property when you have little money.

Another way to get involved in property is with deal sourcing. If you learn how to find property deals and get good at this, you can sell these deals to other people to raise capital. You can save your own earned income by simply moving your expenditure around – for example, by cancelling some direct debits – so you can save more faster. But the second you tell yourself, "I haven't got enough money for property, so I'm never buying property," that's what you'll do. You need to believe first and take action second. It's all about having the mindset of a lion!

Don't compare yourself with me if you're just starting off or even with somebody else, because we will all be at completely different stages. It's taken me years to get to the stage I'm at now. Accept that you need to have a period of learning and experience. In reality, it's unrealistic to attempt to do too much in your first couple of years, much as you might want to.

Go at a steady pace. You can still buy property if you haven't got money, you've just got to find the right way. Obviously, it's easier if you have money. So, aim to get yourself in a position where you can earn more money so you can invest it in property.

I'm a big believer in the power of focus and simplification. Simplify things: if you boil half the things down, they're not that complicated. Set yourself clear, specific goals with a timeline, and a deadline. Then, say them out loud every morning, because you're going to lose interest if you don't.

FINDING THE RIGHT PROPERTY

That famous saying: "location, location, location," is right to a degree. You've got to consider the price. Is it within your budget? There's no point looking at Central London if you only have £50,000.

I'm not saying that you should only invest on your doorstep: I know plenty people who successfully invest out of their area. For me personally, I've always just invested in the North East within an hour's drive of where I live because it's what I know. I know the areas where I live: what's good and what's not. It's important to know your area.

Some places in the North East, for example, you can have one street with really nice properties worth £100,000. Yet, literally the next street behind it is full of drug dealers and the properties are worth £40,000. So it's essential to do your due diligence. Just basing it on an area sometimes isn't good enough.

Do some digging. Speak to a lot of different agents. Don't only take the estate agent's advice who you buy off, because they're trying to sell you the property. If you buy a property off ABC Estate Agents, ring DEF Estate Agents as well and ask them for their opinion too. Would the property rent? What would it rent for? What's the area like? You can look at crime stats and research the area online. You can drive past the house at night and during the day. Check it on a weekend and during the week to see what it's like. Look at the cars on the street: are they all rundown Vauxhall Corsas or are there loads of big Mercs? That tells you a little about it.

With regards to the location, for a standard buy-to-let try, make sure it's close to a good school, transport links or a city centre. But if you're doing an HMO (House of Multiple Occupation), it's got to be close to either business estates, a city centre, a university, a college or a hospital. You don't want to try to create an HMO in the middle of the countryside, because that's not going to work. If you're looking at serviced accommodation or a holiday let, you need to look if there's demand. Is it beside the seaside or is it in a city centre where there are going to be lots of contractors or trades who want to come and rent that off you?

Do lots of research to make sure that the location meets your strategy. A lot of the time, you get a feel for a property. If you go and visit, you will get a feeling for the room sizes. Ask yourself: is the layout right? Sometimes you might go there and think, *Oh, I don't like this.* But you should never buy on emotion. You should never think, *Oh well, if I wouldn't live here, someone else wouldn't live here*, because that's definitely not true.

Everybody has a different perception of what they would live in. I used to think, *Why would someone just rent a room?* But my HMOs get filled up in a heartbeat, within a couple of days of advertising them for letting. Just because I wouldn't rent a room, that doesn't mean other people won't. It's completely the right decision for some people if they're on a contract or if they're in between jobs or new to the area or a student looking for term-time accommodation. So, find the right location for the right strategy. Do some digging and trust your gut.

SWEETENING YOUR OFFER

You may have heard the saying: "You've got to kiss a few frogs." You're likely to view a lot of properties to find the right one at the right price. You make your money when you buy, not when you sell, so make sure you don't get emotionally attached to the purchase. Don't think, *Oh, I really, really want it*, and get in a bidding war. Decide on your buying figure and don't go past that. Negotiate.

Always, always undershoot. Some people say, "Oh, I wouldn't put in that offer, it's too cheap," but I've bought properties for 50 percent off the asking price before.

A helpful tip is to give a rationale for making a low offer. Don't just say, "I want to offer £100,000 on this property please, because it needs a bit of work." That is likely to be shot down in flames. Instead, say something like, "The reason why I'm offering this is that I've looked in the area, and it is really rundown. Have you been in it? It stinks. The kitchen is horrible. It needs a new bathroom and the boiler. It's probably going to need to be rewired. The garden is a state … It needs £30,000 to tackle this – it needs a lot of money spent on it. The area is not the best. That being said, I would still like to purchase it – but it's got to be at the right price. I don't want to offend the vendor in any way but this is the reason my offer is X. I can complete quickly and I will send you all of the ID docs and proof of funds now to show you I am serious …"

There are a few ways you can handle this to take the sting out of it. You can say, "I don't want to offend the vendor in any way, but what do you think would be the absolute lowest he would accept for a quick completion?" If you say that to an estate agent, you'll get a different answer than if you say, "What do you think I can get away with?" or "What do you think I could get it for? Are they a motivated seller?"

The estate agent might say, "The minimum they're going to take is £80,000," So respond by saying something like: "Oh, really? I wasn't expecting to pay that much. Eighty? Seventy is the best I can do." There's no harm in negotiating. Things like "best and final" are not necessarily best and final. The estate agent legally still has to put your offer to the vendor, so when you say "best and final" and lose, you can still make another offer. Don't be scared to renegotiate, because they still have to go back and tell the vendor.

Another thing to make your offer seem more attractive is to have proof of funds. I always send my ID and address to the estate agent while I'm making the offer and I've got them on the phone. I say, "Listen, I'm legit. This is my background. This is what I do. I'm going to send you proof of ID, proof of address, my solicitor's details, and proof of funds right now while we're on the phone. What's your email address?" So then the estate agents think, *This guy's credible. He knows his stuff. He's serious. It's not just a daft offer.* Little things like that help when you're negotiating and they help you get the right property at the right price.

If it's an HMO or buy-to-let, look at likely demand. Go on Rightmove, Zoopla, etc., and look how much stock is in the area. Look what it can be rented out for. Look at the spec of other properties in the area and see what you're competing against. Likewise if it's an HMO, go on SpareRoom.com and look at the demand in an area. Look at what they're renting for and the spec. Do your research.

AVOID BUYING ON EMOTION

Buying a £100,000 property or a £200,000 property is still quite a big investment. You don't want to just make a guess or fluke it. Yes, you want to make an educated, calculated guess, and assess a calculated risk. But let the numbers guide you. Don't buy with emotion, only buy on numbers.

If you have a set return on your investment or a set yield, whatever number that you're looking for, you have to let this figure guide you – not the property or your feelings. Have a number that you won't go past and don't deviate from this. If you've got a minimum yield or a minimum ROI, don't give way on that. You have to stick to your guns and trust your numbers. Let the financials guide you, not emotions.

I learned this valuable lesson from the early properties I bought. You've got to remove the emotion and any pride. Too many people buy on emotion and sell with emotion as well. When you buy a property because you like it, you're not thinking logically.

You should buy property purely on numbers. Let the numbers guide your decision, nothing else. And when those numbers aren't working, you sometimes need to cut your losses and walk away.

"I CAN'T FIND A DEAL"

I sometimes hear people say that they can't find a deal. Sadly, they're lying to themselves. If they can't find a deal, it's most likely because they are being lazy and not taking their own or their kids' future seriously enough. That's the harsh truth. There will always be properties out there at the price that you want to buy for in the area that you want to buy in. There always are.

Everybody in 2020 said there were no properties on the market. Everyone in 2021, was saying that there were no properties on the market. I found 8 in 2020 and 13 in 2021. I deal-sourced 5 as well. So that's 18 in 2021 while other people claimed they were struggling to find one. So why is that? Perhaps they weren't looking in the right places or weren't viewing enough. Or maybe they were just kidding themselves.

I will ring estate agents most weeks to make sure I stay on their radar. In 2019, I sourced 45 property deals for other people and I purchased 16 properties myself – so 61 deals, which works out at more than one a week. In order to do that, you have to view loads of properties. You can't find that many properties without huge action and being good at speaking to estate agents and knowing exactly what they want. Literally, when we found that many deals, one of my colleagues and I were probably viewing 20 properties a week between us.

If you're reading this and thinking, *I can't do that* or *I'm too busy* bear in mind that at the time I had two children, and I also had over 40 staff who reported directly to me in another business. I have multiple other businesses and I still went to the gym and socialised with my friends. However, I still found time.

You might think: "I work 9-to-5." Well, what about weekends or evenings? Have you rung an agent and said, "Can you do an early morning viewing or a late viewing at night?" Or have you actually asked an agent to do a video for you? There are virtual tours online now. You can even pay people £20 to do a viewing for you and record a video walk-around. If it's important enough to you, you will find the time.

So what's your excuse? Because half the barriers most people put in front of themselves are self-created and self-inflicted. So stop it: go and start viewing some properties. It's just a numbers game. The more you view, the more you're going to find. Yes, you might have to change strategy and you might have to pay a little more in 2022 than you did in 2019. But there are still deals out there right now. I'm finding them and I know plenty people who are, too. It's purely down to mindset and taking action.

If you're really new to property investing, remember that just because you've never found one before doesn't mean that you're never going to find one. At one point in my life, I had never found a property before. I didn't come out the womb and run straight onto Rightmove, did I? You can develop any skill with time. Sourcing properties and finding good investments is a skill that you have to develop and work on. So put down this book (but read again tomorrow), get on Rightmove and go look for some properties. It's that simple.

> **Put down this book.**
>
> **Get on Rightmove and look for some properties.**
>
> **It's that simple**
>
> **– but start reading again tomorrow!**

HOW MANY PROPERTIES DO YOU VIEW BEFORE YOU FIND ONE?

When I got started, I had to view a lot more properties to find a good deal.

Now, when I do my research, I filter out a lot of the viewings. But that only comes with time, experience and knowledge. I'll probably get 1-in-4 or 1-in-5 offers accepted now. That's because I don't do a viewing unless I've done the research. I will know:

- the area;
- the type of property;

- the strategy that I will use;
- information about the property.

Most importantly, I've spoken to the agent and I will know if there's a chance of getting a deal. I've usually done all that pre-research before I even view it now, so I've really whittled it down.

I'm often asked how many properties a person who is new to property investing might need to view. I would say for the first few years anything between 10 to 20 viewings would be expected to find one that's the right price for you and your strategy. As soon as you accept that it's going to be a lot of viewings, that's half the battle. Some people, if they don't know this, will view the first five or six, offer on them all, and get a "no" for all of them. Then, they'll say, "I can't do this, I can't find one," and give up. They might give up on the ninth one, when the tenth might have just been the one that said "yes."

If you don't go on the viewings, you're definitely not going to get any property. If you don't ring the agent, you're definitely not getting a property. If you don't try, you're definitely not going to get one. If you keep trying, eventually you will succeed.

Even if you view 100 properties, before you get one that's perfect, is it worth it? That's about 100 hours' work for the viewings, including traveling – 100 hours' work to get a property that pays you and your family forever? It's worth it if you look at it like that.

The choice is yours. You just need get out there and get to work. Do the basics and the things that you need to do consistently, which are:

- research,
- view,

- offer,
- speak to the agents regularly.

That's all there is to it!

I've done a podcast on this on "The Rags to Riches Show with Terry Blackburn" called "How I find volume of property deals on Rightmove". Check it out for more tips on finding deals.

SPECIFIC CRITERIA FOR A PROPERTY PURCHASE

There are different criteria for each property that you buy. For me, if it's an HMO it needs to net £1000 a month. If it nets £1000 a month and I get all of the money that I've spent to acquire and refurb it back within four years, I'll do it. If it's longer than four years, I won't do it.

That's a 25 percent return on investment or return on money left in the deal. The majority of my deals are properties that need work – where I can do a refurb, lift the value and then refinance the property and pull most of my funds back out, but they also then need a cashflow after that.

With most of my deals, I've got my money back within two or three years after the refinance. So then, it becomes a free property. If I get back the money that it's cost me to purchase and refurb, that property is therefore free and cost-neutral. At that time, once I've got my money back, I break even. I've got no money left in, therefore that is free money for me and my family.

So that's what I look for. I make sure I've got my money back within four years maximum. There are holiday lets, buy-to-lets and HMOs.

They all follow those same principles. I've got to have my money back. Some properties don't need any work but are just high cashflow and don't cost that much, so I do those as well.

I bought one just recently that didn't need any work, but it netted £1200 a month. That cost me to about £35,0000 all in to purchase. So it's two and a bit years to pay it off. That didn't need any work which is rare for me. I do like to buy the ones where I can do work, lift the value and then refinance it, but that was an example of a good return. The property was ready: I got it at a great price and it cashflows really well, so I'm getting back the money that I put in in under three years.

That's all that I look at, because my focus is: as soon as the money comes back in, every bit of rent, every bit of re-mortgage money, goes straight back out and is invested in buying a new property. I don't use that money for living expenses. It's income to buy more properties, to build the Blackburn family portfolio.

PULLING YOUR MONEY BACK OUT

Let me break down the mechanics of pulling your money out of a property. The usual process is that you purchase below market value, you add value by refurbishing the property (new kitchen, bathroom, etc.) and then you refinance at the new higher value.

PULLING MONEY OUT OF A PROPERTY

1. Purchase below market value
2. Add value by refurbishing the property
3. Refinance at a new higher value.

So, to break this down: you'll typically buy with a 75 percent loan on the property. Let's say the property is worth £100,000. That's a £75,000 loan, with a £25,000 deposit. Then you spend some money refurbishing the property – let's say you spend £20,000. It's then worth £150,000 after the improvements.

The mortgage lender will let you refinance at 75 percent of the new value – so you'll get the difference between 75 percent of the original purchase price and 75 percent of the new value. If that difference covers all of your money, amazing – it's a free property! It's just cost you a couple of months of time purchasing it and getting it refurbed. If you get your money back in two years, it's then a free property that produces cashflow forever.

The key to it is buying enough below market value and then being able to lift the value enough and then getting a revaluation high enough that the bank will release 75 percent of the new value. This is the key to successful property investing.

CHOOSING TRUSTWORTHY TRADESPEOPLE

It can be hard to get the right team together. I don't think there's anybody out there in the history of property investment who hasn't experienced a bad builder. If someone says to you, "Every builder I've ever worked with is sound. They do everything on time. They've never gone over budget," they're probably a little wooden boy called Pinocchio because I don't think that's possible!

Loads of them will be over-budget. They'll add loads of unexpected things onto the bill. They'll make mistakes or not turn up on site. You can't escape that to a degree. You have to put up with that to find the good ones. You might get lucky and get a few good ones first time around. That's great if you do. If you find someone who you get on with, is trustworthy, is on time, reliable, and doesn't take the pee, hold on to them and treat them well.

Always check their work but pay them on time. I pay all my tradesmen every Friday – none of this 30 days or 60 days after the invoice, because I don't think that's fair. They should be paid on time, as long as they've done the work.

If I can't be there, I get them to send me a video of the work they've done: a picture or video at the start showing the empty kitchen, then a picture or video at the end showing the completed kitchen. Then I'll pay them on that Friday or I'll get some of my team to go around and do inspections. But if people are just starting with you, you do need to go and check their work.

Anybody who's done this long enough will have experienced the text message on a Friday from the builder, while they're in the pub: "I need that money, mate." That's at 9 o'clock, then 10 o'clock, then 11 o'clock. Then it starts to become, "Where's my fucking money? I need my money." Missed call, missed call, missed call. That's what they do.

Use websites like Checkatrade. Builders have to do a lot of vetting to get on there. They can't just register themselves; they've got to almost be interviewed. They go out and meet the traders and check all their certificates and qualifications. The traders also have to get references from people they've done work for. So you're not going to get a cowboy on Checkatrade or other equivalent sites.

Try not to use friends to do the work. At the very start, I used close mates and asked them to do work on the cheap. I know that does work sometimes, but it can also cause friction and affect your friendships. If you've got to tell someone they've done something wrong and say, "I'm not paying you for that," your friendship can be ruined potentially, so be wary of that. The same applies to family.

Don't be worried if a property looks like a bomb site when you view it, because everything can be fixed. It just depends on how much it's going to cost. Every problem has a solution. When you're speaking to builders who say, "Oh, this is a problem and that is a problem," just have the view of, "What's the solution? What can we do? Let's not dwell on the problem anymore." The same applies in business, relationships and everything else. Don't dwell on the problem; dwell on the solution. Be solution-oriented and focused. Whatever happens to you, think: "How can we solve this as quickly as we can?"

YOUR TEAM

SOLICITOR – You need a good solicitor. In particular, you need an efficient **solicitor** who does everything really quickly. Solicitors are the main time delay in purchasing properties by a mile, so you need to have a fast and efficient solicitor. I think there's that much to do in the legal process and the type of people who are solicitors just don't do things in a hurry. They take their time on everything. So you may end up just having to find the best of a bad bunch!

MORTGAGE BROKER – You've also got to have a good **mortgage broker**, ideally someone who understands property investment. A lot of mortgage brokers unfortunately are order takers and they don't have a clue about property development or property investment. They just are used to doing residential mortgages for first-time buyers and home movers. You ring them up about a quirky HMO Grade-2 listed building and they might put you with the wrong bank which will ruin your credit rating – which then, in turn, sometimes even makes you lose the property because it took so long. So you need to find a good broker who understands bridging finance and ideally a broker who invests in property themselves.

I do mortgages in-house. If you contact me, I can put you in touch with my mortgage brokers. I work with guys from other firms who specialise in commercial finance and bridging finance too. I use them because they're specialists and they both are investors so they know this inside out. They can do deals that other people can't because they have access to certain lenders that other people don't. Having the right broker can be the difference between getting a deal and not, so contact me on Instagram if you'd like help with this.

ADMIN ASSISTANT – When you get to a certain level, you will also need help with your **admin**. You can get a virtual assistant for that or someone who works directly for you, employed, to do all your paperwork.

LETTING AGENT – You need a **letting agent,** someone who can advertise your properties properly, take good photographs, market them properly at the right price, and then do all the maintenance and the management and make sure it's compliant with regulations.

A good tip here is to get friendly with estate agents – be nice to them and build your relationships with them so that they'll bring you deals and become almost like your own little deal sourcers who don't cost anything.

INSURANCE BROKER – You'll also need a good **insurance broker** for your landlord's insurance as well. I can also help with this if you need me to – just send me a message on Instagram.

To summarise, you've got to have people around you who know more than you do. Having the right team around you to ask for advice and run ideas past could save you a lot of time and money.

The beauty of the Age we are living in right now is that we have social media and reviews. You can find out a lot about somebody just by checking them out online.

In addition, ask around for word-of-mouth recommendations. Reach out to other people who are doing more than you and ask them, "Who do you use?" Ask for suggestions. Don't complicate it. It's as simple as that.

WHICH STRATEGY FIRST?

If you're new to property investing, I personally think you should do buy-to-let first. Buy-to-let is just one house – ideally a house, not a flat or apartment. Rent that out to one family who will pay a steady amount of rent every month.

I recommend getting a solid base of buy-to-lets first to get some steady income. These are the least profitable deals, but it just gets you used to being a landlord. After this, move on to HMOs.

An HMO is a house that you're renting out per room either to students or professionals. You typically get more rent for one of these. There are loads of books about that explain all the different strategies if you wish to explore these in more detail.

HMOs are a bit more complex. There's more maintenance, heavier refurbs, more regulations and compliance issues. They are just more hassle to deal with in general. After that, look at serviced accommodation as the next step. Then, after that, it's the bigger projects.

There's no clear "right" or "wrong" way to do it, which is what I think a lot of people are looking for. They want to find the right strategy for them or the perfect formula. I don't think there is one. You've just got to decide on one strategy and go with it. This is just the formula that has worked for me and many other people that I know. They started off with buy-to-lets, then moved on to HMOs and serviced accommodation. After that, some people go onto huge developments and conversions or self-builds.

Don't run before you can walk!

PROPERTY FINANCE MINDSET

People who don't have money think, *Why would someone else lend me money?* You're doubting yourself there because some people will. Someone that's got £1 million in the bank would lend you £50,000 if you say the right things. Just because you wouldn't lend somebody that much money, doesn't mean that somebody else wouldn't lend it to you.

The reason why banks lend money on property is because it's safe. There's a well-known phrase that says it all: "safe as houses". The banks don't give you a mortgage on stocks or shares. They give you a mortgage on property because they know it's a secure asset class. They know that there's value in property and it can't go to zero even if there are ups and downs in the market.

It's all about having the mindset of a lion rather than that of a hyena. You might be thinking, *Oh well, I don't want to get loads of mortgages because that's debt.* You need to understand that there is good debt and there is bad debt. Bad debt is things like credit card debt, car loans and debt that doesn't create any more money, that just costs you money, that's high interest. But good debt can be used to create more money and produce an income that covers the cost of that debt plus a surplus.

I'm in millions and millions of pounds' worth of debt, but it's all good debt. I want more debt: I want £100 million worth of debt. This is because £100 million worth of debt will mean £400 million worth of property that will create hundreds of thousands of pounds a month in income. So it's essential to get your head around the fact that not all debt is bad.

Saving money isn't the right thing to do. Paying your mortgage off isn't the right thing to do. Getting debt-free isn't the right thing to do.

Getting bad-debt free is the right thing to do – but not getting good-debt free. Get as much good debt as possible. This is the lion's way of thinking.

Get as much good debt as possible. This is the lion's way of thinking.

Around 99 percent of high-net worth individuals in this world will have lots of good debt – whether that's in a business, houses in their portfolio, on other investments. The richer you are, the more debt you've got a lot of the time. People think that the richer you are, the less debt you've got – but that's not true.

YOU DON'T NEED TO BE GOOD AT MATHS

You don't have to be good at maths to invest in property. I've always been reasonably good at maths, but I've got zero GCSEs. I didn't even do my A levels. I'm a financial adviser, I run a finance company, but I didn't pass maths. What does that say?

Half of what we learn in school is pointless in my opinion. I want my children to do well in school for discipline and social skills more than anything. I'm not really bothered if they know where Jerusalem is or if they can learn all the chemicals on the Periodic Table. I'm not bothered because these are not life skills. People learn how to communicate and socialise in school.

Maths is an important skill, but everyone has a calculator on their phone. So if you're not good at maths, you have a device in your pocket that is good at maths. That's all you need. It's like delegating tasks at work. You're just delegating the sums to the calculator and it'll do them for you.

This goes back what I mentioned earlier in the book about beliefs instilled in you as a child. Just because you were no good at maths or English, or whatever else you've been told all your life, it doesn't mean that you're not going to be good at business or property investment. A hell of a lot of people in property and business left school early or came out with no qualifications. I'd probably say over 50 percent are from that category.

So, no excuses!

KNOWING YOUR 'WHY?'

Things sometimes get tough in life – whether that's in business or property investment.

That's why it's really important to know your big reason "why". Your "why" is your driving force. It's behind everything you do in your life.

You're not going to get up on a Tuesday morning and make a presentation to angel investors if you haven't got a reason "why" you want to grow your business or your property portfolio. Your reason 'why' might be: I want to make history. I want to be recognised and remembered for hundreds of years for what I achieve in my industry and space. Or it might be: I want to provide a better life for me and my family and to buy a new house and start investing so I can eventually retire early.

Mine is that I want my children to have the life that I didn't have, although I'm certainly not going to gift them everything. What I visualise quite clearly is in years to come I'm sitting at a table with my three kids and then their kids at the same table, with my partner Louise as well. So I visualise that table where it's a Blackburn family meeting and we discuss how much the property portfolio has generated for the family this month.

That passive income covers all of my bills, and all of theirs too if necessary. It gives us all a lifestyle that we want and produces a great quality of life for everybody in my family. But there's also a surplus and I want to have conversations with my family about, "What do we do with the surplus this month? Where do we invest it? How were the businesses running this month?" This is a family legacy that's not just my kids, it's my kids' kids' kids. I believe I can create that based on where I am now at 32 by the time my kids have kids. That's probably 20 years away. I want to be remembered for hundreds of years for what I achieve in my life. I mean: why not aim this high, think this big? Someone has to, right?

Writing it down every day and speaking it out loud every day will literally make a huge difference as to whether you achieve it and stick to it or not. You need to have a reason why it's important to you.

Everyone talks about one-year, three-year, five-year goals, 10-year goals. What about 100-year goals? Nobody really talks about that. That is: what do you want for your kids' kids? Because you can start working on that now. For me, I want my great grandkids to say: "Great Granddad Terry started all that: he visualised it and wrote it in a book. He said he was going to do it and now we're living it."

So I visualise sitting at that table with my family in many years to come, discussing what our property portfolio is generating. My kids will have to work—they might want to be paramedics or something else, and that's absolutely fine—but they'll still be involved in the family business in some capacity if they want to be. Then, we'll have them sitting round the table and discussing the family wealth. That's one of my own biggest reasons why.

I also want to make a mark in the world: I don't just want to be like everybody else. I want to be renowned for being very good at business and property and writing books that are motivating and educating other people across the world. So these are huge goals that aren't easily achievable in just a couple of years.

Obviously, I set 12-month goals every year, and I have quarterly goals and mini-goals as well. But I find that the really huge goals are the ones that motivate me the most.

When you set a really massive goal, then you're motivated for a lifetime.

BE A LION: HEALTHY BODY AND MIND

CONNECT WITH ME

Take pictures of your journey as a lion – include photos of yourself; sections of this book that you find helpful; quotes that you like; your list of goals, etc. Then, post it and tag me on Instagram.

THE HEALTH & FITNESS WILDERNESS

The Health & Fitness Wilderness consists of:

Lions

They are super healthy and happy: they look and feel great and walk around with confidence. They eat well and enjoy their lives; they are full of life and vitality, great to be around and always smiling. They have good bodies, good skin and just look overall very healthy.

Hyenas

They say, "I'll never be fit," "I'll never be skinny, I'm big boned," "My genes won't allow me to get a six-pack," "I can't run a marathon, I'm not fit enough," "That person over there must be on steroids," "She looks good, but I bet she's not happy." These types of people just always criticise others for being healthy and try to justify why they will never get to that level. We all know them.

Sloths

These fools don't think exercise is important. They can't get their lazy asses off the sofa to go on a walk, never mind go to the gym. They get takeaways every night and love eating crap. They don't even know what they are putting in their mouths and are generally slobs. Sloths and slobs – it almost sounds the same, so it's a good word for them!

HEALTHY BODY

FITNESS & EXERCISE

Having a lion's mindset is key to health and exercise as much as everything else.

If a lion isn't fit, it's not going to catch any prey.

I want to have a great quality life and live a long life. That's why I look after my health. I don't want to die at 80. I want to be 100+, if that's possible.

Far too many people think that by going to the gym a couple of times a week, they're going to see a huge change. In reality, let's be honest, your mindset has to be: *This isn't a quick fix.* You can't get ultra-fit or have big muscles or have a six-pack or drop a waist size or dress size by just going to the gym a few times but not sticking at it long-term.

Exercise is a continual thing – forever.

If you go to a gym, you will see people there in their eighties and nineties still exercising. It's a continual thing to keep your body in good shape. It's proven in countless studies that exercise is good for your mind as much as your body: it helps you live longer, it helps you feel better about yourself, and it improves your mindset. When you look good and have a nice body, you feel good about yourself.

On the flipside of that, if you're overweight and hate the way you look, that's not good for your mindset. That will then affect how effective you are in other parts of your life. You'll maybe be grumpier with your partner or less tolerant at work, whereas if you feel good you're generally happier and nicer to be around.

There are so many things that everybody knows, but we just don't put into practice. Like we all know that eating junk food and processed food is bad for us, but we still do it. We all know that alcohol and smoking is bad for us, but a lot of people still do it. We all know that exercising is good for us, but we don't do enough of it. These are all well-known rules, but people just don't follow them.

The busiest time at a gym is January, because everyone sets a goal for their New Year's resolution, thinking: *I'm going to get fit.* But they're not in there by February – everybody knows that.

Look at all these daft photos online where you see a "before" and "after" photo and they're selling a magic pill that you take to lose weight. That just sums up a lot of people's mindset, because they want a quick fix. They believe in a quick fix and they'll pay for a quick fix, when in reality there isn't one.

People want a six-pack, but they're not prepared to diet and exercise regularly. That's why some people take fat loss pills, diet pills or steroids, because they want the cheat code. They want the secret ingredient or pill to get there quicker. Everyone wants that quick fix.

So, with exercise you've got to get your mindset around the fact that staying healthy is a continual thing that doesn't stop – because if you get ultra-fit and run an ultramarathon, if you then stop for the next year, you're going to get unfit again. That's just what happens: you have to keep it up.

So exercise is a mindset thing first and foremost.

CHANGING IT UP

A way to help with this is to try not to do the same thing over and again so that it becomes repetitive or boring.

For example, for years I've done weights training like a lot of men do. With weights training: you train your chest and your biceps, and you try to get big. But that gets very monotonous as you're doing the same thing repeatedly. When you do that, you plateau and your results plateau, and you lose your motivation. It's not very exciting. You get to the gym and just go through the motions, do the same exercises with the same weights, just doing the same thing over and over. It's not much fun and you don't even get good results from that.

So for me, with exercise, it's important to change it up. You could do cardio one day, weights the next day, HIIT training the day after, (which is high-intensity interval training). The day after that, you could then do CrossFit and then you could do a walk.

Exercise doesn't need to be an intense full-on two hours long. You could do some yoga. On YouTube, you can get free videos and there's some stretching that is really good for you. You still get a sweat doing some yoga and some stretching sessions. Just mix it up. Or if you're tired, go for a walk; just doing some form of exercise, making sure you're moving enough. It's good for your body. It's good for your heart. It's good for your mind. We all know this, but again most people just don't do enough of it.

If a lion looks unfit, other lions will sense that weakness.

So how do we relate this to the lion mindset? Simple: lions don't mess around. If they want to do something, they just go and get it done. If a lion isn't fit, it isn't going to catch prey; it's not going to eat. If a lion isn't fit, it isn't going to be able to defend its territory. If a lion looks unfit, other lions will sense that weakness in the way it walks, the way it moves. Another fitter lion may even come along and challenge him to a fight and take over his pride. So a lion can never let itself go fitness wise. He always has to be in peak condition physically.

So you need to be fit if you want to catch what you want in your life. You need to be active, fit and healthy, with a spring in your step. You get that by doing a few different things – which we'll explore in more detail in this section – but exercise is a huge part of your life and it needs to stay in your life until you're no longer on this planet.

You perhaps can't do as much as you get older, naturally, but you need to be doing something at least five days a week minimum.

I do change my exercise plans quite regularly to stay motivated. At the moment I'm doing upper body Monday, lower body Tuesday,

day off Wednesday, then upper body Thursday, lower body Friday, and then sometimes I'll do a run on a Saturday. At the end of those upper and lower body sessions as well, I'll do something with a bit of cardio involved, so it'll be like a mini-circuit, to get my heart rate right up. So I'm getting a bit of cardio and weights and I'm hitting every muscle twice a week at least, but I change that up. Sometimes I'll do two runs a week. Sometimes I'll swim. You've got to keep your body guessing and you've got to keep yourself entertained. I have two days off: Wednesday and Sunday.

GAMIFICATION

Another tip to help with keeping fit is gamification – make a game of it. This might be: *"I'm going to exercise for 30 days in a row"* or *"I'm going to see how strong I can get on bench press in the next three months by trying to increase the weight every Monday"* or *"I'm going to see if I can beat the time of my last run."*

Just make up some sort of challenge to keep it interesting. It is really important to keep up your motivation. If you don't, you're more likely to stop doing it.

You have to have a big reason why you go to the gym – whether that's to look good, feel good, training for a bodybuilding competition, or you're trying to lose weight to improve your health. Whatever it is, you've got to have a reason. Gamification is like a mini-challenge that will give you more motivation.

If you just said, "I'm just going to go to the gym five times a week for the next year," that's great. But I think you're more likely to keep it up if you are more specific about your goals, such as, "For the next year I'm going to do x, y and z and I'm going to do it for this many days … and I'm going to achieve this at the halfway point and this at the quarter point."

You will have a better chance of sticking with it and succeeding by turning it into a game.

HIRE A PERSONAL TRAINER

Hire a personal trainer, if you can afford it. This is definitely worth doing, because even if you have a powerful reason why you're doing it and you've made it into a game, there may still be some days where you're lacking motivation.

Having a personal trainer there just to push you on will get the best out of you. Sometimes when you're training by yourself, on the last couple of sets you will take it easier. You'll do a couple less reps or you'll drop the weight by an extra 10 kilograms.

You'll do less, because nobody is standing over you, pushing you or encouraging you. That's just natural. I think it happens to everybody. But by having a personal trainer there, they'll push you on. I strongly recommend that if you can afford it.

Exercise is essential for good health. It benefits not just your body, but it also helps your mind – so it's a must.

YOUR POSTURE AND HOW YOU CARRY YOURSELF

Having a good posture is an essential part of your wellbeing and success in life. If you don't believe me, think about how you picture a really depressed person and a really happy person.

The depressed person is typically slouched. They've got their shoulders forward, their head down, they're looking at the floor and their clothes and hair are usually scruffy. When you slouch, first of all it doesn't look very nice to have a hunched back visually. Also, if you're slouched over, your lungs aren't open properly.

If you think of a depressed lion with a droopy tail and a slow walk, it's also going to look very vulnerable for other animals to take advantage of it. It's going to be instant prey if a pack of hyenas comes along.

So posture is important – both for yourself and how others perceive you.

A depressed lion with a droopy tail and slow walk is going to look vulnerable if a pack of hyenas sees it.

If you want to improve your posture, you need to speak to a personal trainer. My posture wasn't very good when I was growing up, because I didn't do much sport or exercise at all when I was younger. I wasn't really into sports. I was too busy getting into trouble or doing the opposite of what I should have been doing!

But then I spoke to a personal trainer and started correcting my posture by doing things like dead lifts which straighten your back.

Certain types of back exercises will really help with your posture. When you stand tall – head up, chest out, chin up – you look better than when you're slouched and looking down. You feel better. You look better. You walk more confidently. You appear more confident in general.

Confidence is one of the best things you can ever have in your life: it helps with relationships, it helps with work, it helps with everything. If you're confident in yourself and your own ability, people will want to be around you, people will like you, people will be attracted to you.

You don't have to be the cleverest or best-looking person in the world. If you've got confidence, you will attract the people who you want to attract. You'll attract the job that you want and the friends that you want. You'll be able to negotiate deals if that's what you're into and if you're in a sales environment, you'll close more deals. Having good posture makes you appear confident, which helps with everything.

So, if you work at a desk or a computer during the day, have regular breaks. Get a proper posture chair. Don't sit in the same spot, slouched over for too long. Just during recent Covid lockdowns, for example, I felt my shoulders pull forward more. It's not that I wasn't exercising, because I was. But I was at the computer screen a lot more than I previously had been, so I felt my shoulders pull forward a little bit. You just have to correct it by stretching, being aware of what you look like, and correcting this.

Last year, I bought a posture chair and I thought, *Am I really going to pay this much money for a chair?* It was over five hundred pounds, but it really works. It's got mesh material and you can mould it to the way you want, so I don't mind spending the money. I'd rather spend money on something that helps my posture than waste it on something unnecessary. People will happily go and spend £600–£700 a month on a car they don't really need, just to show off. Yet they won't spend £500 on a chair that could correct their posture.

I do a lot of driving, so I consciously try to sit up straight. Don't have your chair leaned too far back or too far forward. Have it up straight and try to sit up straight. Don't let your shoulders pull forward; keep them back with your chin up.

Again, this is a constant thing. It's not like you can just correct your posture by doing some exercises over the space of a couple of months and then forget about it, because it will just go back to how it was.

If you drive a lot or if you're at a computer a lot, you need to get into the habit of having regular breaks and sitting up straight.

So what you have to do is design your life so that you develop habits in all the different parts of your life. Then, you implement them into your life and keep them there forever.

BREATHING

I have been to see a breathing specialist who is certified by Wim Hof. I find it fascinating how something as simple as breathing has all kinds of crazy health benefits. He taught me a really simple breathing technique: "Try to breathe through your nose as much as you can as a habit, because that gets more oxygen to your brain than if you just breathe through your mouth as that's going directly to your lungs. You need to try to breathe through your nose as much as possible."

Sometimes when you wake up in the morning and you're really sluggish, you may find that is because you've been breathing through your mouth rather than your nose.

I've been told that a good habit is to put your tongue to the top of your mouth. If you do this, then try to breathe through your mouth, you can't. You end up breathing through your nose. So, when you go to sleep, put your tongue to the top of your mouth and hopefully when you wake up you should still have it there, because that means you've been breathing through your nose when you were sleeping. That's good for you. Then, you will typically wake up in a better mood and you'll have more energy.

Now I'm very conscious of that. Even when I'm driving I remember: *Tongue to the top of my mouth.* I'm trying to implement that as a habit.

When you're designing your life, you need to implement all of these habits into your working day and the times when you're awake. This will help you to get where you want in your life.

HEALTHY EATING

It's commonly known that eating a variety of fruit and vegetables is good for you. We all know that sugar is horrifically bad for you for many different reasons. We know that too much fat is bad for us. Yet people are still addicted to sweets and junk foods. We all know what's good for us and not good for us, but we all let ourselves off too much.

A lot of people overeat or binge-eat comfort food because they think, *I'll just do it this once.* But then this turns into, *I'll start the diet on*

Monday. Then that becomes, *I'll start it next month.* Then it's mid-year and they're thinking, *Oh, I'll just write this year off. I'll start again in January.*

By giving yourself an inch, you're sometimes giving yourself a mile. People gradually get into bad habits and then it becomes a vicious cycle. They start off unhappy, so they eat junk food and they see that as comfort food. Then, they get more unhappy, so they need more comfort food, so they're in a cycle that's hard to get out of.

Food is fuel for the body. If you fill up a car with cooking oil or beer in the tank, it's not going to run. So don't expect your body to run effectively and be at its best by putting in the wrong kind of fuel like sugar, fat or junk food.

In the past five or six weeks, I haven't drunk any alcohol and I feel amazing. My energy levels are through the roof. Drinking is a social thing to do, a very common thing to do, but nobody can argue that you're not the best version of yourself when you're hungover and you're sharper, more alert, and think faster on your feet when you haven't had a drink. So, because of that, I've made a decision to only drink on special occasions. I used to drink a lot, but my mind has been changed on alcohol just recently.

Going back to diet, on the positive side, you need to eat a balanced variety of fruit, veg, protein, carbs, and fat, depending on what you're wanting to achieve.

If you're wanting to lose weight, you just eat less. It's a really simple logical thing to do: eat less and cut out all of your sugars and processed foods. If you want to get a proper meal plan, then do that.

You can get one online or watch people on YouTube talking about it for free. You don't need to hire a nutritionist or pay money for a fancy diet plan to do this.

I get the majority of my meals delivered because it saves me time having to go to the supermarket to buy everything. The meal prep is done and the calories are tracked, so it's good fuel, but I don't have to think about it.

I want to perform at my best, so I put the best fuel in my body that I can. I'm not saying that I eat healthily every day, because I definitely don't. I will have a takeaway with my partner if we can't be bothered to cook and it's a Saturday night. I'm not that boring that I just eat salads every day!

You can have a day off and a cheat meal sometimes. Though if I know I'm going to have a takeaway or cheat meal, I'll typically exercise on that day. It just lets me off in my own mind!

Ultimately, food is the fuel of your body. So you need to use the best fuel if you want to perform at your best – it can literally help you achieve what you want faster, because we all perform better when we're feeling good.

Dieting is harder than exercising for me, because when you're hungry it's easier to just eat stuff that's not so good for you, rather than prepare something healthy that is.

SMOOTHIES

Often, I use the blender to make healthy smoothies. There are three good reasons I do this. One is to get the calories in, when I've just trained in the gym and I've been awake for three hours. It's a way to get calories and goodness in you quickly.

It's also saving time. If you're wanting to get some good carbs, protein and maybe some fruit in you, then you're going to have to prepare some food. If you make porridge, muesli or something with some fruit and honey for your carbs, and then some scrambled eggs for your protein, that can take easily half an hour.

So all I do is put all my ingredients into a Nutri-bullet: three eggs, a packet of porridge, chia seeds, spinach leaves, fruit juice, fruit (blueberries, raspberries, bananas, apples, pears, etc). I just mix it all up and bang it in. Then, you blend it all up and I drink it with my supplements. So I'll have a multivitamin tablet, a Vitamin C tablet, Echinacea, (a natural herb that is good for your immune system), a cod liver oil tablet, a krill oil tablet, (which is good for your heart), and an iron tablet.

That saves time as I get loads of protein, carbs, fruit and vegetables in one hit.

This is perfect for weekdays when I don't have much time. I've got things that I need to do each day during the week, so it's a quick smoothie blasted in the morning and then I attack the day.

On weekends, I have much more time to make the whole family a nice breakfast.

TIME-RESTRICTED EATING

Intermittent fasting, for me, is a great way to lose weight if that's what you want to do.

You just eat within a window of time. I used to start off with 12 noon till 8pm, then I reduced that to 12 noon till 7pm, then that was reduced to 12 noon till 6pm. You can ease into it if you haven't done it for a while.

You just stop eating at the end time and don't eat anything after that until the next day. Then you eat within that time window again.

I've found that the weight drops off you and comes off your stomach very quickly.

There's lots of research into intermittent fasting, how it's really good for your body, and your mind, and it's linked to living longer. I don't do it all the time, but some mornings I could easily skip breakfast and not eat till 12. Black coffee (no milk, no sugar) curbs your hunger, so does water.

Intermittent fasting a couple of months a year is beneficial. I might do this for a month or three months if I really want to drop some weight.

The majority of the time I'll have breakfast about 8am to 8.30am, after I've done the rest of my morning routine. Then I'll have lunch at 12, a snack around 3pm, then tea at 6pm to 7.30pm.

I try not to listen to too much diet 'advice' – especially if it's trying to sell you a product or service. I take it with a pinch of salt and just try things out to see what works for me. People have different genetics, body types, and goals. So it can never be one size fits all. That's where some people fall down. They'll read something and think, *Oh, I'll try that because that guy got really muscular doing it,* or, *That girl lost lots of weight, so I'll do it too.* But you're not that girl or that guy. Everybody is different, so I think you've just got to find out what works for you. Eating a healthy, balanced diet works and being aware of your body.

Sometimes if I'm a bit tired or lacking energy, I will have some carbs or coffee. But I can tell what my body needs by just being self-aware. If I'm really sore from the gym, I know I need some protein, because weight training tears your muscles. Protein fixes that, so I'll have extra protein that day or some extra sleep. I'll go to bed a bit earlier, because sleep helps with repairing your muscles.

It's about being really aware of where you are right now.

HEALTH CHECKS

One of the things that can help you be aware of how healthy you really are (as opposed to how healthy you think you are) is to get a health check.

I go to the Nuffield Hospital and get a check-up every year. When I went the first year, the consultant told me, "You're very healthy. There's not one thing wrong with you. Your blood pressure, lung capacity, BMI, everything is absolutely spot-on. There are no health issues whatsoever. You probably don't need to come back for another five years." But I said, "I'm still going to come back every year," because they might pick up early signs of something that I can fix. I'd rather know than wait five years.

It's around £700 for a full health check, but everything gets checked. They make you run as well as getting on an exercise bike. They check your lung capacity, and do loads of tests on your nerves, your muscles, your eyesight, your hearing, etc.

At the end of the day, if you want to perform at your best, your body needs to be at its best. If I have to pay £700 every year and it helps me live an extra 10 years and it helps to keep me illness-free, then it's worth it. You can't put a price on your health.

WATER

One thing I do as soon as I wake up, without fail, is drink some water. We're made up of around 80% water, so it's natural you should need to keep topping it up, especially if you have been sleeping or working out.

I've always got a big three-litre gym bottle attached to my hip everywhere I go. I've got two in the office. I've got one in my home office. I've got one upstairs in the house and one downstairs in the house. I've got one in the car; one in my gym. Much to the annoyance of my partner Louise!

I make sure I drink loads and loads of water, because it's good for your body and your mind.

I used to think that I needed coffee to be alert 100 percent of the time when I'm awake, but if you drink enough water, that has a similar effect. When you drink a lot of coffee, you crash and then you need another coffee to pick you back up.

However, if you drink enough water throughout the day, you feel very alert. Start to drink two to three litres of water a day minimum. Watch the difference in how you feel. I feel like this all the time now, because I always drink that much water. If I don't drink enough water, I feel tired and sluggish, so I have to drink more to pick me back up. I sometimes drink four to five litres a day.

It's linked to all kinds of health benefits. I think the main cause for headaches and migraines, which a lot of people suffer from, is dehydration because you're not drinking enough water. You can also gain weight if you don't have enough water as you tend to eat more. You are also more likely to have brain fog and feel more tired. So, it makes you more alert to have it, which is probably why a lot of schools are encouraging kids to take water bottles into class with them. At the end of the day, it's a no-brainer. Again, it's very well-known that water is good for you, but many people just don't drink enough of it.

It doesn't really matter whether you drink tap or bottled water. I just have big bottles of water everywhere in the house so there's no excuse for me not to drink it. In my car, I've got a huge multipack of bottled water. In the office, I've got a bottle. I take them wherever I go. If I'm going to the shops, I've always got my water bottle. Even when I'm driving, I'll have a drink in the car. It's so automatic now, I hardly have to think about it.

Again, it's about building a new habit into your routine so that it becomes a part of your lifestyle.

NIGHT-TIME ROUTINE

Nobody can deny that if you have a bad night's sleep, you're not your best the day after. You're usually sluggish. You've got a headache. Your eyes are sore. You're not your best.

So you need sleep – quality sleep.

It's about listening to your body and working out what's right for you.

I'm not as strict and as disciplined with my night-time routine as I am with my morning one. My night-time routine is typically to try not to look at my phone towards the end of the night. Unfortunately, with the world we live in, it's very difficult to stay away from your phone. I find it especially hard as I run multiple businesses and have loads of staff, so it's always "ping, ping, ping" constantly. But it helps to stay off electronic devices for at least an hour before bed.

I try not to eat too late. I personally find that if I eat late, I don't get a very good night's sleep. It's just not a nice feeling if you go to bed on a full stomach. So I try not to eat after 7.30pm to 8pm at the latest. After that, I generally try to relax and take my mind off the day. If you're up early, work all day, then work all night until you go to sleep, again and again, you're going to end up ruining your health and also very lonely. Maybe you'll end up rich, but you may also end up dying younger. You don't want to work yourself into the ground. Life isn't all about work.

So my night-time routine is: having my tea; settling down and relaxing, trying to take my mind off work, speaking to my partner and kids. Sometimes I like to read a book while I'm winding down. Then, I'm usually in bed by 9.30pm to 10pm every night.

This is what I like to do and it works for me – going to bed early and getting up early. That's the way for peak performance in my experience.

I think the number of hours you sleep is down to you as a person. If you need eight hours, then have eight hours – though I wouldn't recommend any more than this, because you don't want to lounge around all day like a sloth.

Personally, I like to go to bed around 10pm, and then I'm up at 5am. I do that five days a week but not on weekends. On the odd morning, if I am feeling tired, then I give myself an extra hour or so. I might get up at 6am or 6.30am, but I'm never up really later than 7am Monday to Friday.

I think a lot of people as they get older need less sleep typically. You just have to be aware of your body and not be too hard on yourself. If you're absolutely exhausted, don't force yourself to get up at 5am.

I often hear people say things like, "I'm a night owl. I work better at night." If that's actually the case that's fine, continue to do it. But, in my experience, the people who say that have never even tried to get up at 5am. They might have tried it once, but then they're exhausted and think, *I can't do this*, so they don't try again. I was like that the first time I got up at 5am as well. But then when I did it regularly for a couple of weeks, I got in the habit. You eventually get in the swing of it.

I'm sure there are successful people out there who work late and are really creative at night and get up a little bit later and that's fine. But you have to work with your own rhythms and do what's right for your body.

Just make sure the time that you are awake is productive and you're not wasting it.

MORNING ROUTINE

The reason I get up so early is I am up before my kids and my partner. I come downstairs, have a coffee and then I do the following things. I must credit my good friend Tom Smyth for this, as he told me what he does each morning and I applied most of it and changed a few things. It really, really works for me:

- I write my mantra: the things that I am and I want to be.
- I practise gratitude: I think about the things that I'm grateful for in my life.
- I state my goals: what I want to achieve.

I do this every morning and then I exercise for 45 minutes to an hour and, if I've got time, I'll read. Sometimes, I'll do a little less exercise or a little less writing to get some reading in. I'll then go and get ready, have a shower, have my breakfast. That's typically all before 8am.

So when most of the world is just getting ready and getting started, I've already done a lot by then. This, for me, eliminates that excuse of "I don't have time to ...."

This is the main excuse I hear: "I don't have time to do xyz ... I have a career. I have kids. I have loads going on." These are just excuses. If your day is so busy you can't get any exercise in, you need to get up earlier or change your schedule, because if you're too busy with work to exercise that's not going to last, because you're going to work yourself into the ground. If you're working that much that you can't exercise, it's probably going to ruin your health or your relationships. So you need to change that.

You can do everything and have everything. Just as a lion does what he wants and has what he wants, without anything holding him back, you also can. You can have the life of your dreams if you want and design it that way. It all starts with a shift in mindset.

MORNING WRITING RITUALS

A good morning routine sets you up for the day ahead. I'm now going to explore my morning writing rituals in much more detail so that you can copy them too.

YOUR MANTRA:

For my mantra, I always write: "I am so happy and grateful now that…" at the top of the page. Then, I will write things that I already am in addition to things that I want to be and what I want to be known for.

So this might be things like:

- I'm an amazing father to my children.
- I'm an amazing partner to Louise.
- I'm an amazing leader to all of my staff.
- I own a thousand properties.
- I release a book that inspires millions of people worldwide.
- I win multiple awards in business, property and for my books.
- I'm an amazing businessman and I achieve huge things every single day, week, month, and year.
- I'm happy and healthy in every way.
- I am strong, fit, flexible.
- I am a juggernaut – I am unstoppable.
- I am efficient and effective in every part of my life.
- I earn millions of pounds every single year.
- I live the life of my wildest dreams filled with abundance in all areas.
- I'm happy, healthy, wealthy. I love my life."

So, the statements always start with "I" and they are always written in the present tense as if they have happened already.

You should never phrase anything as: "I would like to earn this much money." Instead, it should be as if it is already happening.

So, it's almost like an affirmation, but I call it a mantra. Then, at the bottom of each section, I write: "It's already done". Then, I tick it and sign it: "Terry Blackburn" as if it's happened already. It's like a contract with myself. By signing it, I'm reinforcing all the things that I already am, that I want to be – that I will be. It's like I'm already there.

I write list this every day. Sometimes, if I'm a little bit pushed for time, I'll read out yesterday's to save time. Ever since I started doing this, the things that have happened to me have been unbelievable. It's definitely had an impact because it reminds you what you want. It's about making a big commitment.

It usually takes an hour every day to do my writing rituals, because I write a full A4 page of mantras, a full A4 page of gratitude, and at least two A4 pages of goals. So it's a lot – and it hurts your hand. You're likely to get an aching pain in your wrist when you first do it!

I used to write affirmation cards at the start of the year along with my goals and I would say them out loud in the mirror. Eventually, you memorise the words. So then, you're not really engaging your brain that much by just saying them out loud every morning.

By writing them fresh every day, you're forcing your brain to think, *What else do I want to be? What else am I already?*

Sometimes health may be the most important thing on your mind. Sometimes your family may be more prominent. Then, you're having to physically write the words, so you're having to engage with thinking about what you want most.

When I've shared this with some people, they've sometimes said, "Bloody hell, I couldn't do that every morning. I don't have time." Yes, it is a big commitment. But I'm committing to doing this because I'm committing to being successful in every part of my life and this helps to get me to where I want to be. So if you want a similar result and want to change every part of your life, then I'm showing you how to do it.

I didn't invent this technique myself. I just copied it from another massively successful person. At the end of the day, I'm not Einstein. I'm just putting my own slant on techniques that massively successful people already use.

GRATITUDE

The gratitude part of your list is the things that you're grateful for. At the top of the paper, I put: "I am so happy and grateful for my…"

Then I will write a list such as:

- Happy, healthy, kind, beautiful, children.
- Amazing, strong, happy, healthy partner, Louise.
- Amazing relationship that is full of love, laughter, fun, happiness where we support each other and are the perfect fit for each other.
- House that I live in.
- Clothes that I wear.
- Properties I have.
- Amazing team I have around me.

I write anything that I'm grateful for on the day. Sometimes if you've had a great night with your partner that might be your dominant thought. Or you may have just seen your kids' school play or sports day, so it's more about them. Or it may be more about your body or your health or financial stuff.

Whatever comes into your mind at the time, just write it down. The point of listing your gratitude is so you'll attract similar things into your life in future. So if you're grateful for your body, you're probably more likely to then eat well and exercise, because you're telling the world and yourself that you're grateful for it.

Again, at the bottom, I always write: "It's already done," tick, and then sign it.

GOALS

Nobody gets excited by the idea of an average life. You don't get any sense of success, achievement or progression if there are no exciting goals to inspire you. If you're just coasting through life, there's nothing to work towards or work for.

To get you up in the morning, you need goals. It doesn't have to be: "I want to become a billionaire." It could just be: "I take my partner out once a week and we have an amazing relationship." That's a goal that'll keep you focused, because you need to do something every week to achieve it. Goals are like signposts along the track of life. You can go down different paths, but goals keep you on the track that you want to be on and get you to the destination where you want to be. You can have enjoyment and fulfilment along the way by setting these goals. I truly believe that progression towards achieving your goals is a big part of happiness and how happy you are.

Many high-performers and high achievers write down their goals. If very successful people do that, why aren't we all doing it? The more you write down your goals and the more you say them out loud, the more likely you are to achieve them rather than forget about them.

You have to be relentless. It's non-stop and never-ending. There's a phrase that relates to goals: If you're persistent enough you'll get it, but if you're consistent enough you'll keep it. You've got to be persistent *and* consistent with your goals which takes time and practice.

With goals, it's about being really specific, and clear about what you want. So it's not: "I earn a £1 million" because that's not detailed enough. Instead, it would be: *"I earn £1 million per year every year from 2022 onwards. This is a combination of my salary, dividends, business sales, business acquisitions, property income, book sales, coaching and everything else I'm involved in. I deserve this level of income and it flows to me with ease."*

A goal has to have a deadline. It needs to be specific and have detail, because the universe loves detail. The clearer you are, the more likely it is that you will attract it.

Again, to illustrate this point, I could just write: "I own a thousand properties." But instead, I would put: "I own a thousand properties on my 45th birthday. This produces over £600,000 net profit per month. This puts me in the elite one percent of high-net worth individuals in the world and I start to mix in these circles. I am backed by hedge funds, huge organisations, and individuals. I use all kinds of different strategies to purchase properties all over the world." Then: "It's already done." Tick: Terry Blackburn.

So, I write around five lines on A4 paper for each goal – they're very detailed which is why it takes so long to write them.

It gives you a boost of energy when you write down all the mantras because they're so positive. Gratitude gives you a sense of calm, inner peace and happiness, because you're writing down things that you're grateful for. Then, the goals fire you up, because it's all the things that you want and are excited about.

SAYING IT OUT LOUD

There's a special ritual I do after my writing exercises. I stand in front of the mirror and shout my goals out loud, really loud, every morning. My daughter often comes in when I'm doing them. She just stands by my side and looks up at me.

The first few times she saw me doing this, she asked, "What are you doing, Daddy?"

When I told her, she said, "You're silly."

But she keeps watching, not every morning, but some mornings she'll come in.

I'll say,

"Remember that one? How long have I been saying that one?"

"Ages."

"Well, that just happened."

She's only eight, so she doesn't fully understand. But she's starting to realise that if you say things out loud with emotion, with passion, with enthusiasm and energy that they start to happen. She's seen it for herself.

I also know these things do come true if you say them out loud, Because you're tricking your mind into believing that everything you're saying has already happened.

Examples might be:

- "I am the best of all-time in financial services."
- "I am a multi-millionaire."
- "I own 100 properties."
- "I am an award-winning property investor."
- "I write a best-selling book."

Nearly everything that I've ever put on one of those cards that I really meant has happened.

Most people don't even know what their goals are. They think they've got them in their head, but they haven't. Let me ask you: can you actually, hand on heart, remember what goals you set for yourself for your last New Year's resolution or the one before that? If you didn't write them down, the chances are that you can't.

Some people can't even remember last week or month, never mind at the start of the year. You can't because life gets so busy and runs away with you and you get caught up in all sorts of other things.

So why would you remember a goal that you didn't take seriously at the start of the year?

But if you wrote it down and you shouted it out loud every morning, it will be at the forefront of your mind. You're constantly reminding yourself of it.

Let's say, for example, one of your affirmations is that you sell to 10 clients per week, every week, in 2022. Every morning, you would say out loud, "I sign up 10 new clients per week." If it's a Wednesday and you still haven't sold to anybody, you're far more likely to pull your finger out and make it up in the remainder of the week.

By constantly reminding yourself, you know that you'll take more action: you'll call more clients, you'll do more prospecting, you'll make more phone calls, you'll do more social media advertising. You'll push because you're telling yourself every day that's what you're doing. Therefore, you'll change your habits and behaviours by constantly reminding yourself of your affirmation of your goal. So writing your affirmations and saying them out loud is massively important.

Once I've done my writing rituals, and said my affirmations out loud to the mirror, I go to the gym. There, I blast my music while I'm training to get in the zone and finish my exercise. This way I've got all the endorphins rushing so my mind and body are sharp before I even have breakfast.

THE POACHERS

A word of caution here: be careful who you share your dreams with.

Of all the lion's enemies, poachers are the most lethal.

Poachers are similar to hyenas in a way. They fully are the people who seem intent on killing a lion's dreams – for trophies or some other twisted reason. These poachers are naysayers who will try to hold you back. They will try to suck out any the good vibe or energy that you have. They will come at you with spears of hate or bullets that you don't see coming, to try to kill your plans stone dead.

If one of these small-minded people gets wind of your ideas, they'll try to kill it straight away. They'll tell you that you can't achieve it: "How are you going to do that? Don't be so ridiculous. You'll never do that." Because they aren't happy themselves and have never achieved anything, they project their negativity onto you. They try to make your life as desperate and bleak as their own.

As you grow and become more successful, you'll find that you actually start to attract them. Well, it's actually more like they are attracted to you: they try and make their sad lives better by making yours worse. What motivates them, I don't know, maybe jealousy or envy. So, be careful who you mix with and share your dreams with.

If you can, learn to spot them and identify them early. Avoid them and give them a wide berth. Hyenas tend to be motivated by selfishness and self-interest. Whereas poachers seem to be motivated by hatred, spite and a desire to kill dreams. They will try to encroach on every area of your life if you let them – business, health, personal life – even when they have little experience themselves.

So, spot them early and avoid them like the plague.

HEALTHY MIND

The hyena blames everyone else for the problems in their life.

STRESS

It is inevitable that sometimes you're going to wake up and feel like you can't be bothered. Sometimes you're going to feel overwhelmed with everything that you've got going on in your life. Sometimes you're going to feel down.

Stress is inevitable. It's how you deal with it that matters.

Going back to my "shit stick" analogy earlier in this book, the more things you take on and the bigger things you achieve, the more likely you are to experience problems and challenges. What's more, the problems are likely to be bigger. So, if anything, stress is a sign you are on the right track as you progress in life. It can't be all rosy and go your way all the time!

To cope with this, it helps if you can just accept there will always be problems mixed in with the amazing times. When something happens to make you feel stressed or worried, train yourself to automatically think, *What's the solution?*

For example, you might have loads and loads of different things on—property, businesses, family issues, personal issues, relationship issues. If you're focusing on, *Oh, this went wrong, that went wrong*, you're giving your energy and your attention to the wrong thing. So when you feel stressed, train yourself to think what the solution might be.

The fix might be: *I've taken on too much. I need to either get some people to help with this or I need to delegate more or get rid of some of the things that are on my workload.* If you're stressed about your partner because they're dragging you down, then perhaps you've got to consider changing your partner. If you're stressed because you've put weight on, then maybe you need to eat better and do some exercise. If you focus on the solution rather than the stress, then you're much more likely to overcome it.

Sleeping on a problem often helps. Sometimes when you're really overwhelmed, just getting to bed early, dusting yourself off, starting again the next day is the best thing to do. It certainly helps me if I ever feel like that. Sometimes, another useful technique is just thinking to yourself, *Is this problem really worth me feeling crap about all day? Is it worth ruining my whole day?* Half the time, when you think about the problem logically, it's not. If you can be disciplined enough to do this, then ask yourself, *Is this problem even worth 10 minutes of my time?* Again, half the time it isn't. So you realise, *Why on earth am I letting it impact on my day and other parts of my life?*

Stress is linked to loads of different types of illnesses ranging from heart disease to cancer. So you need to make a decision whether you want to be stressed or not and how long you stay stressed for. If you feel stressed, ask yourself, *What's the solution to not feel like this any more?* You can never stop stress completely, but you can reduce it by your life choices and who you choose to have around you.

Design your life to have minimum stress. Here are some things that will help you:

- You've got the right partner.
- You've got the right team around you.
- You're looking after your health.
- You've got a business you love.
- Your business can run without you.
- You've got income that comes in no matter what.

These are some of the main factors that will minimise the amount of stress you experience.

So design your life so that you reduce the likelihood of stress.

BE SOLUTION-FOCUSED

Being solution-focused is a great technique for dealing with the daily challenges that life sometimes brings. Negativity, rejection and knockbacks are all part of life. They happen to every single person on the planet.

The lion's mindset is about being solution-focused, rather than problem-focused.

The lion's mindset is solution-focused rather than problem-focused.

So, whatever happens, try to have a mindset of: *What's the solution? How do I fix this?*

For example, your business is collapsing, about to go bankrupt. *What's the solution? Could we sell it to somebody right now? Could we resolve this? Could we get a funder? Could we get an angel investor to help?*

There's usually a solution for the majority of problems whether they are professional or personal ones. You get diagnosed with an illness. *Who is the best expert to ask about it? What's the medication? How can I get better?* Exercise, eat well, drink more water, get your mind right, meditate, write your goal down of getting better, take the medicine.

For 99 percent of things, there is a solution. So ideally, you should just get in the habit of thinking, *I've just had a big knockback. What's the solution? What could I do differently next time?* It will help you to take the lesson from the experience and think, *How do I make sure that I don't do the same thing again, so this doesn't happen again?* It's about learning too. If you keep getting the same knockback repeatedly, it's a clear message that you need to change. It's about taking responsibility for your life rather than letting yourself become a victim.

If your relationships keep ending up in the same way, it might be you. If you keep failing in business repeatedly, it might be you. If your weight keeps yo-yoing, it's likely to be you.

I think that comes down to accountability and taking responsibility for your life. Sometimes you have to be self-aware enough to think, *You know what, it's me and I need to change.*

We live in a blaming culture. People blame other people. "It's his fault"... "It's the industry's fault" ... "It's the Government's fault" ... But that's not focusing on the solution.

The hyena blames everyone else for the problems in their life. The sloth is slower to react and probably doesn't even know what's going on. The lion will always look for a solution.

The lion will always look for a solution.

MEDITATION

It was Ray Dalio's book *Principles* that first influenced me to try meditation. He's one of the biggest hedge fund managers in the world. He came from nothing, but now he manages a fund worth tens of billions. It's crazy what he's achieved. Yet he still finds time to meditate twice a day.

That spurred me to do the same, because I thought, *If someone as busy as that has time to meditate, why aren't I doing it?*

So then I tried it myself. I use the Calm app. which has a daily meditation for 10 minutes. I do it early morning at least three times a week. I don't think I've ever felt overwhelmed or had a bad day on a day after I've meditated. It gives you clarity of thought, calmness, peacefulness. You just centre yourself and forget about all the noise that's going on in the world. As a result, I make decisions more clearly. I don't rush into things; I don't feel flustered or overwhelmed. I just glide through the days when I meditate.

Sometimes if I am feeling a bit stressed, I meditate that night when I get in from work. You can even do it at work. If you work at a desk, take 10 minutes during your coffee break or go to your car. If that 10 minutes helps you make decisions better for the rest of that day, it's definitely worth it.

So, for me meditation is an important part of my life, especially doing as much as I do every day. I have multiple businesses in multiple industries, alongside keeping fit, eating well, managing staff, buying properties, selling life insurance, looking after my children, being a good partner, speaking to my family. I could still do what I do without meditation, but I know I'm better at running my life when I meditate.

The Calm app is around £50 a year I think, but you can also get guided meditations on YouTube for free. In many ways you're killing two birds with one stone as there are law of attraction meditations that focus on things that you're going to attract – so you're doing affirmations and visualisation at the same time as meditation, which saves time.

There's a misconception that you have to spend an hour meditating, which puts off a lot of people. You don't need to do an hour every day: you can do one or two sessions of 10 minutes. What's more, you don't have to sit with your legs crossed on a mat going, "Ommm!" or sitting on a rock on the top of a mountain. You can just sit on your sofa or in the front seat of your car.

If you want to take this a step further, you can also buy a meditation pod. It's a capsule-type pod that you sit in: it's got calming music or you can link it to play music from your phone. You can get one that pumps oxygen or essential oils into the capsule, with light therapy, cues for breathing, and all sorts of quirky things. There's an extra room in the house I just bought and we haven't decided what we're going to do with it yet. So I think we're going to build a sauna and put a meditation pod on the other side. Insta pictures will be on when I get one!

Investing money in yourself is worth every penny, especially if there are health benefits and it helps you perform better at work.

THE POWER OF ENTHUSIASM

Who wants to deal with someone who's not enthusiastic?

I bet every person reading this book has been rung on the phone at some point by a caller with a really monotone, grumpy voice. Instantly, you paint a picture in your mind of what that person looks like. You might think, *Oh, he's miserable. He hates his job.* You literally paint a picture in your mind based on tone of voice and nobody wants to deal with that miserable, unenthusiastic, negative person who hates their job. In other words, a hyena! So you most likely won't listen to what they say or may even put the phone down.

No one wants to deal with a miserable, unenthusiastic, negative person – a hyena!

The flipside of that, is if you get a phone call from somebody with a really nice tone of voice that's bubbly, positive and enthusiastic. You're much more likely to deal with that person than the miserable person.

In sales, a miserable person doesn't even get past the first minute, because you've instantly judged them and thought, *I don't want to deal with this person.*

My point is that it's important to be enthusiastic about everything that you do.

Literally everything. Your relationship, the gym, eating habits, work, money, property, family.

If you're enthusiastic about everything, you'll attract more of the right kind of people to you. People will want to be around you and want to work with you. People will want to be in a relationship with you.

Everything gets better if being enthusiastic is one of your values.

VALUES

Values are personal to each one of us. They are something we tend to take for granted and not think about much – until we meet another person who either has the same values as us and we resonate; or someone who has the opposite values to us and we clash!

One of my values is that I want to be successful in everything I do and that's important to me. I also want to be a good father and bring up my kids well.

I want to make a lot of money, not because I want to keep all that money, but because I want to provide housing for people and do good with my money, as well as creating a legacy for my children, grandchildren and great grandchildren.

Everyone's values are different, but they should always involve being a kind and nice person, having energy and being enthusiastic, because these are things that are important in life.

What are you values? Jot a list down of the things that are important to you.

WHAT ARE YOU VALUES?

Write a list of the things that are important to you.

RESILIENCE

Challenges are always going to happen in life.

Sometimes the lion will run after the gazelle and the gazelle will get away. That doesn't mean the lion thinks, *Right, that's it, I'm not eating any more. I'm done with gazelles. I'm going to starve forever. I'm never going to hunt again.*

Lions don't think like that. They go again on to the next one and the next and they don't stop. That's what a lion does – and that's what successful people do.

Sometimes the gazelle will get away. The lion doesn't give up. It dusts itself off and tries again.

A hyena, in contrast, is likely to give up after a rabbit gets away. Instead it looks for lions' leftovers rather than catching a meal for itself.

A hyena eats lions' leftovers rather than hunting for itself.

Successful people don't give up on something just because it didn't work the first time. They don't stop if they chat up six women and don't get any offers accepted. If they go to the gym for a month and haven't got any stronger or fitter or lost weight, that doesn't mean they stop.

In every part of your life, you have to be resilient. There's not one person on this planet who has every single thing going their way every single second in every part of their life. People like that don't exist. Everybody has to deal with rejection, with negativity, with things not working out.

So, learn to dust yourself off, carry on, and try not to let it bother you. If it's big knockback, a good night's sleep often sorts out a lot of things. Maybe you could even get counselling if you're going through a really difficult time – there's no shame in that whatsoever. If you feel that you're really down, go and speak to somebody about it and get help. Find a counsellor or a therapist. I think there's more courage in doing that than not doing it.

PEAK PERFORMANCE

To maintain peak performance in all areas of your life, you have to make sure both your mind and body are at their peak first. This will help you to perform at your very best both physically and mentally.

So, everything that we cover in this book will help with this:

- Writing down your goals and achieving them every year.
- Practising gratitude.
- Knowing your values.
- Meditating.

- Reading.
- Educating yourself.
- Exercising.
- Eating healthily.
- Drinking water.
- Surrounding yourself with the right kind of people.

To give yourself ongoing support and motivation, you can: get a mentor; join mastermind groups; get involved with people who are similar to you or doing more than you. This then fuels your ambition, your passion and enthusiasm for what's possible.

Being structured and organised also helps you to maintain peak performance:

- Having written goals for the short, medium and long-term.
- Having to-do lists.
- Prioritising important and non-important, essential and non-essential tasks.
- Organising and structuring your day.
- Focusing on one task at a time.
- Delegating and outsourcing.
- Eliminating non-essential tasks.

That's peak performance – enabling you to be the best version of yourself.

Self-development is never-ending. I am always trying out new strategies as well as tweaking old ones as I go. For example, I am continually writing down new goals and replacing the ones I have already achieved. After I won the Investor of the Year Award in

2021, I'd already changed my goals by the following morning. It wasn't even 12 hours after I had been to the awards ceremony, and I'd already doubled the goal that had won me that prize.

My point, going back to peak performance and peak state, is about having a lion's mindset and being relentless. Yes, I'll celebrate for a few hours, but then I'll set a bigger goal that is going to take twice as much effort. You never stop. A lion is constantly pushing on towards the next big thing in all the different parts of life.

A lion is constantly pushing on towards the next big thing in life.

This can be a health goal, a fitness goal, a holiday goal, a family goal, a relationship goal, business goals, property goals, financial goals. You have to be relentless in your approach to everything you do. The second you've achieved something, you can celebrate for a day, but then you set a new goal.

Without a goal you're just stagnant – a sloth sitting in the same place, in the land of complacency, half-asleep and getting nowhere.

Without a goal, you're a sloth sitting in the same place, half-asleep and getting nowhere.

PHILANTHROPY

Giving back is really important. There's no point making hundreds of millions of pounds and keeping it all to yourself. If you've got a million, you can afford to give away a good few thousands. If you've got hundreds of millions, you can afford to give away a few million. Look at some of the most elite wealthy people in the world and they're all giving away most of their wealth.

I give to multiple charities on a direct debit. I've also held a gala dinner every year for the past four years and we always try to raise some money for charity there. I want to do more as I grow in my career and to set up my own charity eventually.

I also want to help other people with my message that anyone can be successful no matter what their background. There are many people who are less fortunate than me, maybe they've had illnesses or they're homeless or they've had a drug addiction or whatever. I want to give them a message of hope and set up a charity at some point to help them.

I think it's important to give back as your career progresses. However, I see charity as more than just helping people – it is about teaching them to fish rather than just giving them fish. So it is not necessarily just about handing over money. It's about giving education to people who need help to turn their lives around.

LIFE BALANCE

When people talk about work-life balance, that implies that work should be half of your life and life should be the other half. I think this is wrong because, of course, there's more than two parts to life.

There's health, relationships, investing, hobbies, sports, etc., to name just a few.

You can still achieve a balance of say 10% each, but you've got to set up your life to be that way. Again, you've got to believe that you can achieve this first.

Loads of people think you can't be both wealthy and healthy because they believe you don't have time to go to a gym and run a business. As I've been explaining throughout this book, it's a mindset shift. First and foremost, you've got to believe that you can.

Ultimately, you've got to be disciplined when you set up something in your calendar. If you say, "Every Wednesday I'm going to have date night," no matter how busy you become, you have to stick to that. If you're picking your children up at 3pm on a Tuesday, no matter what comes up, that's what you have to do. No cancellations.

You have to be very disciplined because you will often feel like you have far too much on. Then, the easy option might be to ask your partner to pick up the kids from school or make them tea. I could very easily say, "I've just seen this massive property that I need to do the numbers on. It's quite time-pressured. I need to act within a day to get this deal." But my children are my priority.

So learn to have different priorities at different times of the day. During the day, obviously work might be your priority. (Though if you are at work and there was an emergency with your kids, obviously you would drop everything.) But usually, whatever task you're on, that should be your priority at the time. This is the sort of focus that will enable you to find balance and get things done.

Occasionally, your life balance can go haywire. When you're starting up business, for example, work can sometimes be 70 to 80 percent of your life. Staying disciplined and setting a structure that you stick to is hard to do, but essential.

STRUCTURING YOUR TIME

I've got a Google diary/Google calendar, so I put absolutely everything in that calendar—when I go to the gym, meals, when I go out with my friends or partner, when I have the children, my work appointments, my viewings with property. Every single thing that I do is in there: you can set recurring events that are the same every single week. I try to be really structured—I go to the gym and have the kids at the same times each week—because the more routine you've got, the easier it is to structure your life which means you can do more and be efficient with your time.

We all have exactly the same number of minutes, 24 hours a day, seven days a week. Yet some people achieve so much more in that time than others. They don't have any more time: they don't have an eight-day week or a 26-hour day. They just use their time more efficiently. You can do this too by having a diary and being strict with your time.

Years ago, if I had an hour-long appointment, I used to always overrun and thought nothing of it. But think about it: even if you have an appointment and the overrun is only 15 minutes, if you've got six overruns during a day, you're an hour and a half behind by the evening. So, if you have to pick up your kids at the end of the day, your free time has all gone. By being a little bit late consistently, the knock-on effect even in one day is a couple of hours.

So you have to be disciplined with your time. If it's a one-hour phone call and you've got another appointment straight after, just end that call bang on time so you can get onto your next one.

Everything else in life is the same. If you've got an hour to train and do some exercise in the morning, be strict about timekeeping. I put my headphones in, because I don't really want to talk to anybody in the gym and get distracted. But sometimes they'll come up to me and try to chat. I just say, "I'm really sorry, but I am in a bit of a hurry. Nice to see you again. Bye." Because if I chat for 15 minutes, I either run late or I end up having to cut my workout short and I don't want to do either. We all know those gym goers who love a chat. I think some people go to the gym to chat and socialise more than work out. That's not me – I'm there to do a job, not chat!

This same rule applies whatever you are doing – whether you are visiting the dentist or going to a parents' evening at school. So learn to be strict with your time.

PEAK PERFORMANCE

If you want to perform at your best, you have to feel your best physically and emotionally.

So that literally comes down to:

i. Exercise – Have you exercised? Everyone feels good after exercising.

ii. Self-improvement – Have you listened to an audiobook or read something to feel mentally at your best?

iii. Healthy diet – You're likely to have brain fog or feel sleepy after eating sugar. You won't feel at your best if you're hungover.

iv. Hydration – You'll feel less alert if you haven't had enough water to drink.

v. Looking good – You perform better and have a spring in your step when you look great.

vi. Meditation – meditating helps with clarity of thought.

vii. Happy home – If your home life is good, you'll feel better. It doesn't matter how well you are doing at work if you come home to a horrible environment.

viii. Teamwork – Life is always better when you have a team that has your back.

KNOW YOUR TRIGGERS

Most of the time, I'd give my mood a score of between 8 and 10. But there's still the odd day when my mood dips.

If that happens (which isn't very often) I know what my triggers are. So I can take action to remedy that.

What you need to develop is being self-aware and identifying your triggers, such as:

- *Am I tired at the moment?*
- *What have I been eating?*
- *Is this person making me unhappy?*
- *Is that situation having a negative effect on me?*
- *Is it something else?*

In short, you need to be able to take a long hard look at: *What's really going on for me?*

Have an early night, if necessary, to feel better the next day. Or if you're unhappy with work or your relationships, take steps to change whatever it is. Change your diet or ramp up your exercise routine. You have to be self-aware enough in order to make the necessary changes.

PEAK STATE

If you apply all the methods I'm sharing in this book, you can achieve peak state the majority of the time. Now, imagine the compound effect of performing at your best every working day! You could retire 10 years earlier, you could get to your financial goals much earlier – maybe even 5 or 10 years earlier!

So do you want to delay your success or speed it up? By performing at your best you will speed it up, because you'll get more done and achieve more when you feel your best. So, I think it's a really important thing to do. You've got to design your life in such a way as to ensure that it's going to happen.

Basketball star LeBron James spends $1.5 million a year on himself to ensure peak performance, I've recently read; so did Kobe Bryant. LeBron James knows his body is his most valuable asset. So he pays for a nutritionist, chefs, massages, a personal trainer, mindset coaches, physios to feel his best and play basketball at his best. He sees this an investment, because he'll make a bigger return if he can play in the NBA for the longest amount of time possible.

Fighting champion Conor McGregor also spends millions of pounds on his body and has a big support entourage around him. He's got coaches for everything—striking, grappling, wrestling, mindset, nutrition, personal trainers—to ensure he's at the top of his game.

So, if you want to be the best businessperson that you possibly can be, how much are you spending on yourself? What are you doing? What are your habits? What are your behaviours? Who are you getting your advice from? And how can you up your game?

HOW CAN YOU UP YOUR GAME?

What are your habits?

What are your behaviours?

Who are you getting your advice from?

A really simple tip for performing better is to speak to someone who is ahead of you in your industry and ask what they do. Then, just copy their habits and behaviours. Half the time, the reason why they're ahead of you is they're doing certain things that you're not.

But maybe you should be!

BE A LION: RELATIONSHIPS

CONNECT WITH ME

Take pictures of your journey as a lion – include photos of yourself; sections of this book that you find helpful; quotes that you like; your list of goals, etc. Then, post it and tag me on Instagram.

THE RELATIONSHIPS WILDERNESS

The Relationships Wilderness consists of:

Lions

Those who have amazing relationships with their partner: they are in love, they are best friends, they laugh together and have fun. They are faithful and have an amazing life together. They give their partner the love and attention they need and their values are the same and they have long, happy, healthy relationships.

Hyenas

There are unfortunately many people like this in the relationship part of life. These are the people who regularly cheat on their partner, who lie and manipulate their partner, and treat them badly. They hold them back from their dreams and prevent them from being who they want to be. They are always being negative about their partner. They regularly end relationships and get divorced.

Sloths

These are the lazy people in relationships who don't really give their partner any attention. They don't give their partner the things that they need, neglect them and don't ever make an effort with them. They are generally slow, lazy people who aren't really enjoyable to be around a lot of the time. Again, this usually ends up in break-ups or divorce – if it's not too much effort!

RELATIONSHIPS — YOUR PARTNER

You could be really attracted to someone and want to rip their clothes off, share similar interests, and even have a good laugh with them. But if your values aren't aligned, there will always be arguments.

This is something that I've only learned since I've been with my current girlfriend, Louise. Before Louise, I got it wrong in relationships, for sure. With both my previous main relationships, there was attraction and we also got on the majority of the time, but our values were different.

For example, if someone's value is that family is more important than business or making money, but you put equal value on making money and family, you will clash.

It may be important to you to push really hard and work late for the benefit of your family. But your partner may see business and money as less important. They may therefore be likely to say things like, "Why are you always at work? Will you stop working so much? You're not bothered about the family, are you? You don't need to buy any more properties. You don't need to grow the business any further. Will you just come home early today? I want to have a date night."

It's not that they're nagging you. This just comes from having different underlying values of what you think is important. This is why couples clash. This is what you want to avoid.

Another example would be if you really value your health and you think fitness and eating right is really important. But your partner might not think this is important. You might say: "I'm going to start this healthy diet. For 90 days I'm going to eat clean." However, your partner might cook you a pasta or bake you a cake with loads of carbs or want to get a takeaway. They might say: "One chocolate bar doesn't matter. One cheat meal won't hurt." Or they might say, "You're always at the gym. You never spend time with me." These are the type of things that people say when they're out of alignment. It's because you don't share the same values.

For some people, it's really important to spend time with friends who they grew up with from school. However, their partner may not have as many friends or may prefer to focus mainly on their relationship. So, again you're likely to clash if you're used to seeing your friends once a week. Even if your personalities match, you make each other laugh and you get on, arguments are going to bubble because your underlying values aren't the same.

Your values around money are another big issue to consider. Loads of people think you go to work, you get a pay cheque, you get a steady job, you get a state pension, you retire. If your partner is like that but you want to set up a business and go self-employed, there are going to be arguments, because they are thinking about security while you are thinking, *I want to take risks and get ahead and achieve big things.*

It's also really important that you are aligned when it comes to bringing up children. For example, whether you raise your voice at them or put them on the naughty step. Some parents don't do any discipline and think, *I had a father or mother who was a disciplinarian, and that was horrible. So I'll let my kids do whatever they want.* On the other hand, you might think, *Kids need structure and discipline.*

So, with relationships, you've got to try to get as many of these underlying, important values in alignment as possible. Eventually, sexual attraction and looks fade, but values don't. So if you're with somebody just because of the way that they look and you're completely different people with different values, that is going to end in disaster the majority of the time.

THE HAVE-IT-ALL MINDSET

My partner Louise and I have very similar values. We're both into business. We're both into property. We're both into health and fitness. We're both into self-development. We both meditate. We both read. We both listen to audiobooks. We both want to bring up our kids the same way. We both want a lot of big things in life. For so many years, I thought there wasn't anybody like that. I was almost resigned to the fact if there was someone with 60 percent shared values there, then that would be fine and I would just settle.

I think a lot of people just settle for what they've got. As a result, there are loads of unhappy relationships. That's reflected by the fact that 50 percent of marriages end in divorce. So before picking a partner and committing, getting married, having children, or buying a house, etc., try to work out the values of the other person. You only do that by having a conversation about what you both want from life.

Don't do this on the first date because you'll probably scare them off. But you do need to find out what their values are. If they're very different in a lot of ways, there's a high probability it's not going to last.

I'm certainly not a relationship guru, but I think a lot of what I'm saying is pretty accurate and makes sense.

I've heard friends say, "You can't have a girlfriend who's also your friend because you can't have a laugh or go out for a drink with the really pretty ones." This is just a stupid mindset that some people have, because they don't believe that you can have it all.

Instead, you should aim for a have-it-all mindset of, *I'm going to find someone who I fancy and who I get on with, who I can also be friends with*. Looks fade. Then what? We need to share values.

I think some people realise what I'm saying too late when they're already married. They've then got to get divorced and experience all the heartache that comes with it. So it's better to realise early on in a relationship. If you're young or single and you're reading this, then fantastic: you've still got time. If you're already married and if you're not with the right person, then you've got to either try to make it work or change it.

Your relationship with your partner is fundamental to success in other parts of your life. It's not something separate and apart from it. Having the right or wrong partner will impact every other area of your life.

YOUR KIDS

My kids are eight and four right now. Parenting is a funny balance, because with children you want to be their friend. But I believe the most important part of being a parent is to make your kids into good adults, and that's very different than being their friend.

If you're spoiling them and trying to please them all the time without giving them any discipline, that won't be good.

Many parents are like that because they want the best for their kids and want to give them all the nice things in life. But is that really making them into good adults? By spoiling them, that can end up having a really negative impact on the way they are as adults, because then they might end up expecting everything to land in their laps and lacking a work ethic. They might turn into really selfish people who just think, *I need to get what I want and fuck everybody else. I'll do whatever it takes to get what I want.* So it's essential to teach them values.

I think one of the most important things you can teach your children is to be kind to others. If everybody taught their kids to be kind and share, the world would be a better place. If everybody was kind, tolerant and considerate, there would be less fighting, less racism, less discrimination and other horrible things. Children don't have any concept of skin colour or disabilities. They'll be friends with anybody at school. But if their parents are racist or discriminatory in any way, the kids pick it up. If their parents are rude to waiters in restaurants, they'll pick it up. If their parents swear at other drivers when they're driving, the kids will absorb it. They model themselves subconsciously on their parents. It's not necessarily just what you say to them, it's how you act and what you do.

A lot of kids have got really good memories. They remember everything. Even if they don't consciously remember, it's still imprinted in their minds. Everything that you say and do impacts them and shapes their life. It moulds them into who they eventually become.

Sometimes it can shape their entire life, because some people aren't self-aware enough to change the habits that they've been given as a child. Whatever you give them it sticks with them forever and they never change. For others, they keep some of the habits and behaviours of their parents, but they're self-aware enough to change the rest. A handful of children turn out completely different to their parents. But you don't really know how they're going to turn out, so as a parent your role is to do the best you can to help them become the best adults they can be.

So I think it's essential to teach them to be kind to others and to share. But I also think that teaching them about money is a must. I don't mean teaching them to become a millionaire or business owner or property investor as that might not be what they want to do. But a really important lesson is the concept of earned income versus passive income. This is never taught in schools and probably never will be – a lot of adults don't even understand the concept. So you need to teach your children the difference and help them understand how things work in the adult world.

Another thing with children which most people won't think of: teach them how to sell. Teach them how to sell Mix-Ups and chocolate bars at school. Teach them how to sell their old toys at car boot sales. Teach them how to speak to people and interact with them, because this is a far more important skill than how to use a Bunsen burner. I don't know about you, but I've never used a Bunsen burner since studying science; I've definitely never re-read *Of Mice and Men* either. It's far more valuable to teach kids skills such as how to sell and earn money.

Getting your children into exercise is important too, because obesity in children is a growing problem. You don't want them to be that overweight child at school who unfortunately in this day and age gets picked on. It's best to teach them good habits with their eating and exercise at an early age to create a healthy pattern for when they are adults.

So your aim is to give them good habits, good behaviours and good discipline, that set them up for life.

YOUR FRIENDS

Everybody grows up with a group of friends that they've known since school. From the successful people that I speak to, there are not many people who are successful in their field who are still friends with only that original group of people and never speak to anyone apart from them. I'm not suggesting that people should never speak to all their old friends again because that's not right. But I think there's a reason why successful people drift away from their roots a lot of the time.

The reason is you that you grow. As you grow as a businessperson, as a human, as a partner, as you develop in your career, other people will grow in other directions too. Some people will just stay where they are and not move, so they'll be closer to a sloth than anything else. They'll choose the safe route instead of the risk-taking route. Others are like hyenas who are constantly watching others, to see if they can snatch or steal some scraps of their success.

Sloths tend to stay where they are rather than taking risks.

That's why you inevitably start to drift away from old friends, perhaps not even intentionally. You start to hang around with people who are on the same wavelength as you, who have the same types of goals. The conversation is different between millionaires and billionaires. It's different between millionaires and people who are on the dole or collecting benefits. If you're a successful person and you're hanging around with people who don't make much money, a lot of the conversations are going to be out of sync.

If you're making £1 million a year, you can't talk to your friend who's on benefits about the investments you want to make, the places you want to go and the things you want to do. They're likely to think you're showing off or put you down and say things like, "Why do you need that much money? Don't you think you should slow down?" Whereas your attitude might be, "No, I don't actually. I think I'm not doing enough. So stop trying to judge me and tell me what to do based on your own limiting beliefs."

Hyenas watch others, to see if they can snatch or steal scraps of their success.

A friend who's doing more than you is never going to tell you to stop doing too much! If I went to a billionaire and told them what I'm doing, they'd probably say, "Have you thought about doing this? Why don't you do this? Maybe you could do that?" They are not going to say, "You'd better slow down, you know, you're doing too much." They're never going to say that because they've been where I am and they've surpassed me and are already on the next stage.

So, often with friendship groups, you'll find that you naturally drift away from childhood friends. You might be really lucky if there are friends from school who are also achieving a lot and flying high. That's amazing if so. Stay with those people. But remember that if you hang around with alcoholics, you're far more likely to have a drink. If you hang around with gambling addicts, you're more likely to have a bet. They'll prevent you from going to the level that you want to be on and may even drag you down to a similar level to them.

So don't forget your roots and who you are. Don't neglect your school mates because you have a lot of shared memories. But do hang around with people who are ahead of you and where you want to be, who are achieving the things that you want to achieve, because they will be the ones to push you on.

A business owner might be doing £2 million a month while you're doing £2 million a year. If he tells you, "This is what I do each month," just copy him. But you only get to learn things like that by networking, making new friends, and hanging around with these types of people. Reading books is great and you should definitely do that. Watching YouTube and listening to audiobooks is also excellent. But hanging around with someone more successful than you – sitting in a bar or a coffee shop, playing golf, going to the gym, etc – will get you inspired. These types of friendships will help you move forward.

The saying, "show us your friends, show us your future," is true. If you don't know anybody who's ahead of you, message them on social media and compliment them: "You're in the same line of work as me. I look up to you. You inspire me. I'd love to take you for a coffee if you could give me 30 minutes of your time." Some of them will ignore you. Some will say, "I'm too busy," or "Let me come back to you." But some will say yes if you ask enough.

If you want to do big property development, ask someone in property who's doing big developments. Make it easy for them to say "yes": "I'll drive to you. Can I come and meet you or can we arrange a phone call?" Networking events are another way to meet successful people face to face.

Some people put blocks, hurdles and barriers in front of themselves which just aren't there. Just message them. So what if you get rejected by some of them? Eventually you'll find someone who's friendly and happy to meet you.

When I first started the podcast, "The Rags to Riches Show" I interviewed the billionaire Alfie Best who I mentioned earlier in this book. I just messaged him on Instagram, got chatting to him, and asked if he wanted to come on the show. I look up to him: he's achieved so much from nothing. Some people might think, *He'd never come on a podcast that's only three months old.* But if you don't ask, the answer is definitely "no".

The moral of this story is stop thinking "I can't". Just ask the question. Ask people who are more successful than you for help and advice. Take them for a coffee or food and start to mix in new circles.

DESIGNING THE
LIFE OF A LION

CONNECT WITH ME

Take pictures of your journey as a lion – include photos of yourself; sections of this book that you find helpful; quotes that you like; your list of goals, etc. Then, post it and tag me on Instagram.

LION LIFE DESIGN

THE 90-DAY PLAN

I'm hoping that by reading this book, it will give you a kick up the bum to copy some of my methods and use them yourself too. The best way to establish a habit is by committing to doing something for at least 90 days. If you commit to doing this and get to work, watch what happens in 90 days, because your life will massively change if you stick with it. (You can also buy my "Be A Lion: 90-Day Journal" that goes with this book on Amazon, if you'd like to commit to this).

Lots of people won't. Many people will buy this book, do what I recommend for maybe a couple of weeks and then stop, because they don't have the grit or the determination. They'll then look for excuses why they can't do this, instead of the reasons why they can.

In life insurance, one of the industries I'm in, we ran a seminar recently. We got a couple of the women up on the stage to talk about what they do. One of them said, "Listen, I've got three kids. I'm pretty much a single parent." A lot of people might say because they have kids that's the reason why they can't be a top performer. But this particular woman was one of the top life insurance salespeople in the country. And she explained to us, "My kids aren't the reason why I can't compete with the top performers. They are the reason why I do."

So, it's all about a shift to having a lion's mindset. Stop letting things hold you back and saying, "I can't do this because of my kids" or "I can't do that because I'm too busy working." Your kids are the reason why you should be setting up a business, growing a property portfolio and building your passive income not the reason why you can't.

THE 'EVERYTHING' MINDSET

To design the life of a lion, you first have to believe that you can have everything.

To design the life of a lion, you first have to believe that you can have everything. You can have health, wealth, businesses, property, a great relationship, a great family life, be fit, eat well. You can do all these things at once – all at the same time.

But if you want everything and you want that dream lifestyle, you have to be prepared for a lot of hard work and disruption in your current life, at least initially.

If your life is nowhere near that right now, you have to be prepared to literally rip it up and start again. It's not easy, but this is a big thing. Nothing big is easy to do and nothing amazing is easy to do. You might have 30 years, 40 years, 50 years left of your life. If you want the life of a lion, if you want to be in full control of your life, then you have to do this.

It's a big thing that you're trying to do, so it's going to be hard.

Initially, it's going to be difficult and there will be lots of stress and tears. Your subconscious mind will be telling you, "I can't do it. I don't know if you can do all this." All the things that hyenas and sloths might tell you, your own mind will tell you. A lot of people think, *I'm not smart enough to earn £100,000 a year* or *I don't know how to buy 100 properties* or *run a big business.* You may feel scared at the idea of coming down from the tree. It may feel safer to cling on tight to what you know.

You may feel scared to down from the tree. It may feel safer to cling on to what you know.

But remember this: when we're born, God doesn't stamp everyone's forehead with ink saying: *You're worthy. You're unworthy … You're rich. You're poor … You're fit. You're unfit.*

Everyone is the same when they are born. So if you stamp yourself with any words, you've done that yourself. If those words say, "I can't do it" or "I'm unworthy" then that's what's likely to happen. But that will be your own choice.

You're not unworthy. You are worthy of whatever you want. You can do it if you want. You can have it If you want it.

The only unpredictable element is that some people might achieve things faster than you.

But who cares, as long as you do what you want to do and get to where you want to be?

KNOW WHAT YOU WANT

As we covered earlier in the book, in order to get to what you want, you've got to know what exactly it is that you want. I know that's a really simple thing to say, but some people haven't really thought about it in enough detail.

You wouldn't walk into Sainsbury's and say, "Can I have some groceries please?" They would say, "What exactly? There's a lot to choose from!" If you left it to them, you might end up with a basket of food you would never want to eat. The sloths might end up with a pile of bones. The hyenas might end up with a heap of leaves. And all the animals would go hungry!

Be specific about what you want or you might end up with a pile of bones and go hungry!

So you need to decide exactly what you want on your shopping list. The universe will then deliver, if you back it up with action and belief. So you've got to be really clear on what you want in every part of your life.

So your goals and aspirations about the life that you want need to be as detailed as possible. It all starts by just getting a pen and paper and starting to write. Exactly as I do in my writing routine each morning.

In no particular order, you just need to categorise what you want. Here are some suggestions for headings following the ideas shared already in this book:

- Business.
- Income.
- Investment.
- Relationships.
- Physical Health.
- Emotional Health.
- Fitness & Exercise.

Let's start with health first and look at a more detailed example of how you will put this into practice:

"I want to lose some weight."

- How much weight do you want to lose?
- When do you want to lose the weight by?
- How are you going to measure this?
- Are you going to use scales?
- Are you going to measure your waist?
- What are you going to do to achieve this?
- What exercise are you going to do?
- How long are you going to exercise for?

- How often are you going to exercise?
- What food are you going to eat?
- What foods are you going to avoid?
- Where will you get the food from?
- When are you going to prepare your food?
- How are you going to stay motivated?

So, with each separate goal that you have, state the specific things that you need to do to achieve it. Then, when you know the things that you need to do, build them into your diary and take action every day – consistently. Eventually, over 90 days, this will become a habit. It's simple, but it's definitely not easy. It's very hard to do actually.

TAKE ACTION NOW:

i. Find out what you want.

ii. Decide how you're going to get what you want.

iii. Put it in your diary.

iv. Do it.

I am conscious that if you are thinking, *I need to change every single part of my life*, you may be feeling overwhelmed at the prospect of trying to do a million-and-one things. So, once you have broken this down into categories, just do one thing at a time from each category.

Don't try to eat well, train more, improve your business, and leave you partner all at once! If you try to change too much, you will either feel overwhelmed or you won't be able to stick to it. So try to do one thing in each area of your life to make progress.

Prioritise. For example, if you're massively overweight and that's impacting all other parts of your life, it might be that you focus on getting your health right first before you make a start on anything else.

Then, once you have built that into your working week, do two things in each category and then three things.

There's no right and wrong way of doing this, but as long as you're making progress that's a good thing. If there was a one-size-fits-all list, everybody would have an amazing life by now and be living the life of their dreams.

An important point to remind yourself of continually is that everyone who is now at the top once started at the bottom. There is no elevator to the top floor. You can't just press a button, step in a lift and go up twenty-one floors of success without any effort. You can't go from the bottom to the top quickly. Everyone would like to think that you can, but you have to take the stairs. You have to go step after step after step after step. All the little steps eventually take you to the top.

It may be tiring as you climb up each flight of stairs. At each level, you might pause and take a little break and recharge before you go up the next flight. It might take you 10 years to walk up all those stairs. You might crawl or get out of breath. Or you might be able to run up some flights easier than others.

But one thing is for certain: you'll get to the top if you keep taking the stairs.

PASSIVE INCOME

Far too many people give their earned income more attention than their passive income.

We looked at the difference between earned and passive income earlier in the book.

Just to be clear, I think you should work harder on your passive income than you do on your earned income. At very least, you should certainly be giving them equal amounts of time.

This is because your passive income is your legacy and your inter-generational wealth; whereas your earned income is just your wealth.

Passive income may take the form of:

- Business.
- Rents from property.
- Royalties from a book.
- Affiliate marketing / multi-level marketing.
- Dividends from stocks and shares.
- An e-commerce store.
- An online course.
- A paid membership site or newsletter.

If you can, set up a business or go self-employed or get yourself in a position where you're paid on your results. If you're just getting paid a fixed amount to turn up or you're getting paid per hour, there's only so far you can go with that.

A lion never thinks, I'm not good enough to eat two zebras today.

If a lion has just eaten a zebra but he's still hungry, he doesn't think, *You know what, I don't think I'm a good enough lion to eat two zebras today. I've already had one. I'm being greedy.* If he's sitting under a tree, relaxing in the shade, then he sees another zebra, he'll still go after that zebra because he has no restrictions. He doesn't put barriers in front of himself.

You should treat your life the same. It's not: *I can only have one property. I can only have one business. I can only get so fit. I can only lose so much weight.* You can achieve whatever you want and living that life of a lion is exactly that. You can have everything that you want; and as much of it as you want. You can do what you want, when you want, with who you want. That's what a lion does. That's the entire concept of designing your life. You choose what you want to do in your life, rather than letting life choose what it wants to do with you.

I've talked early in the book about the importance of writing down your goals, prioritising, and putting everything into an online diary. Don't have a hardback diary, because you'll lose it or spill coffee on it or drop it in a puddle. You need to have an online diary that's accessible on multiple devices—on your laptop, your phone, your iPad, everywhere. You live from that diary and you get ultra-structured, ultra-efficient and you put everything in it.

First set up a default diary. On Gmail you can put diaries overlapping each other, so I've got my default diary which is what my ideal week would look like, and then I've got my actual diary over the top of it, so then when I click on a day or look at it as a week, you can see what I should be doing and what I'm actually doing.

For example, I have Motivational Mondays where I do all my sales training with my team: I do catch-up calls with my key members of staff. I then plan for the week ahead and I do some property networking in the evening. If I ever find myself with nothing to do, all I do is I look at my default diary—what should I be doing? It just helps you stay focused and pulls you back to what you should be doing. This saves you from drifting off track during the day and getting distracted with the mundane tasks.

Think about the analogy of a taxi driver. He makes his money when the meter is on, not when he's driving in between jobs. He can get in his car and drive wherever he wants, but he only makes money when there is a passenger in his car and his meter is on. So you need to decide when your meter is on. You need to decide, *If I'm doing sales, when is my meter going to be on?* Because you can't sell for 40 hours in a week constantly. You can't have appointment after appointment every single day all day.

You've got to decide when your meter is on and when your meter is off for every task.

A lion has no restrictions: he doesn't put barriers in front of himself.

OUTSOURCING

I recommend that you immediately start to outsource the tasks that you don't enjoy in both your home and work life. Think how you can remove the low-income or low-fun tasks from your life. Yes, you will still have to do some things that you don't enjoy, but the majority of them can be outsourced.

I don't agree with Tim Ferris's book *The 4-Hour Work Week* which says that you should outsource absolutely everything. I don't think that's possible and it's unrealistic to think to yourself: *Oh, I'll just work 4 hours a day and be successful.* You need to work at least 6 to 8 hours minimum, 5 days a week, in order achieve anything big in my opinion.

Some people say to me, "Why did you get a cleaner? Why would I pay someone else for something that I can do? Why would I pay them £15 an hour when it only takes me an hour?" To which, I would ask you to consider your hourly rate. If you get paid £20 an hour and pay a cleaner £15 and you go to work, you're still £5 better off. Or you can spend the hour with your children or take your partner out for a meal or socialise with friends or go to the gym, or maybe do some self-development. The question is: is your health worth more than £15 an hour?

You can also ask your cleaner to do your washing and ironing then hang everything up in your wardrobe in colours so it's easier to find.

You can outsource all sorts of tasks these days. For example, you can get a gardener or a car valet or even a personal shopper. There are apps where you send photos and someone will buy your clothes for you. You don't even need to think: *what do I buy or not buy?* You can ask them to put the clothes in your wardrobe in day order – so on Monday morning everything will be prepped for you. You can also get people who will pack your suitcases ready for traveling.

You've got to be wealthy to have your own chef or a driver, but what you spend you save on time. If you get a chauffeur to drive you to places, then you can work while you're in the car. Time in the car is dead time unless you listen to audiobooks or you're ringing people and doing work calls whilst you're driving.

Really wealthy people get a helicopter instead of driving. Why? Because it gets them to where they want to be faster so that they can achieve more. There are so many things that you can outsource or delegate. It just means a change of mindset.

Yes, you can hire a personal chef to cook for you. But there are other alternatives for saving time on meals if you're eating at home. You can buy raw ingredients for meals ready prepped, chopped and weighed out – which saves you time on shopping, food preparation, cooking, and planning a menu for the week. You can also buy nutritionally-balanced or calorie-counted meals that are already cooked. Ready-prepared meals don't have to be unhealthy and they don't have to cost a fortune either. There are lots of options to help you outsource this task so you can be more productive with other things.

You may meet some hyenas who just don't get it. Some people will say, "Lazy git, getting a cleaner!" My response to that is: "What are you talking about? Why wouldn't you want to get a cleaner?" Personally, I don't like cleaning and I'm useless in it. So why wouldn't I get a cleaner so I can achieve more in other areas of my life?

There are loads of things you can outsource – either with real people or electronically. I use an online diary that alerts me 10 minutes before every appointment, for example. Or you can hire a PA to structure your diary and book all the meetings in your day.

You can achieve so much more when you outsource things. Six hours of organised productivity is way better than 12 hours of wishy-washy, unstructured time, floating through the day.

RECHARGING

I'm a big believer in having holidays with your family or friends, because I think this helps you to get more done. Let's say if you worked 52 weeks of the year with no holidays. Then, let's compare this to if you worked 48 weeks of the year and had four weeks' holiday. You'll actually get more done in 48 weeks than in 52.

This is because in the run-up to a holiday, you tend to cram two weeks' work into one. That week before a holiday, you get loads done. Why? Because you've put a big time pressure on yourself. Better still, when you're back, you're recharged and full of energy. You're feeling: *I'm raring to go again. Let's attack this week. Let's get loads done.* Taking a holiday is good for both your mental health and physical health. If you're spending time with your partner or kids, it's good for your relationship and family. It's just good for you all round to have time off.

I'm a big believer in having time in the sun. Before Covid-19 came along, I used to have six holidays a year. When I go away, I use the time to recharge. I always read a book and listen to audio. I exercise and have nice food; you get big doses of Vitamin D in the sunshine and feel great. I'm absolutely on fire when I get back from a holiday, because I'm so recharged. If I have six weeks' holiday each year, it feels like I'm gaining 12 weeks.

I wouldn't advise anybody to work every day, every week in the year. I don't think that's healthy. You'll probably end up rich, but you'll end up lonely and probably with health problems as well. So, set aside special time for your friends, family and children especially for things like Christmas, Easter, birthdays and special events. Otherwise, why are you working so hard? Money's pointless if you can't spend it on the people you care about.

Enjoy your money and enjoy your life when you can. Don't get caught up in the hustle and grind seven days a week. I work very, very hard, but I still have time off. Again it's not about either-or, it's about having everything. You can have time off as well as running businesses and doing everything else.

YOU CAN DO IT!

It happened for me, so I know it can happen for you. I'm nothing special. I'm just an average person who came out of school with no qualifications. But I massively believe in myself and I made the decision to have it all. I practise what I preach.

All this stuff I'm talking about – everything in this book – I do. I've done it now for the best part of 12 years. I've trialled and errored all these strategies to get my life to where it is now.

Now, after all the hard work, I'm living a life of abundance in every way. I'm doing what I want, when I want, with who I want. I am living the dream – in a great position financially, with my friends, with my partner, with my health, my children. Everything in my life is good, but that just comes with time. You're not going to get there overnight, but I'm living proof that it can be done. I know I'm not the only person who can do this because I know multiple people who are doing better than me in many different walks of life. There are most likely hundreds of thousands of people who, like me, have done this all over the world. If they can do it, you can too.

Where you are right now – with health, finances, relationships, etc - - is because of your habits, behaviours, and choices in the past. They've got you to where you are now. If the thinking that you have right now was in alignment with where you want to be, you'd already be there. So if you want to stay put where you are right now, just keep thinking and behaving exactly the same way. Therefore, if you want to change your life, it requires a change of thinking. But if you want a different future, you have to make some big changes and evolve as a person. You need to think differently.

That's why I have been doing self-development for the best part of 10 years and I don't think I'll ever stop. I spoke to somebody on my podcast the other day called Immanuel Ezekiel. He's had multiple businesses. I think he's bought and sold over £100 million worth of property in his career. He told me he has spent half a million pounds on self-development and he's still got coaches and mentors now. (You can check out his podcast episode with me on "The Rags to Riches Show with Terry Blackburn" on Apple Podcast,)

Self-development doesn't have a deadline on it. It's not about thinking, *I'm going to read this pile of books or do this self-development course,* then stop. It goes on forever. You have to constantly keep growing and evolving. If you want the life of your wildest dreams, you have to work for it. If this was easy everybody would have this life, but they don't.

STAYING ON TRACK

Don't allow distractions to get in your way. The second anything distracts you, become very self-aware. For example, if I know that something is hindering my success, I'll just instantly cut it out. I'm ruthless about it: I literally walk away in mid-conversation if necessary. If someone's whinging or moaning on, I just say, "Will you please stop!!" People are taken aback by that sometimes, but I just refuse to let negativity into my life. If something is wasting my time, I move away from it.

It's about being disciplined. For example, what is the point in watching Netflix? Some people come in from work and they'll watch *Hollyoaks, EastEnders, Coronation Street.* All the time it's polluting their mind and giving them a false sense of what's real and what's not. They think that life's actually like that and then they start to look at their own partner and they think, *I want my partner to be like that person on that programme.* But these are just actors and invented characters. If you're saying, "I've got no time to set up a business alongside my job," but you're watching three hours of Netflix every night, you're lying to yourself.

In addition to cutting out distractions, you can get up earlier in order to get more done. Sometimes when you find yourself lacking motivation or your focus is drifting off, a dead easy trick that I use is to just write your goals down again. There are plenty of times when I really can't be bothered to go to work or to go to the gym or to view 10 properties in a day.

But now I'm aware every time that a sloth-thought creeps into my mind about, *Just stay in bed today, Terry. You don't need any more property. Let's do it another time.* Or a negative hyena-thought like: "I'll never get that property at the price I want. It's not worth going to a viewing."

Become aware every time a sloth-thought creeps into your mind.

As soon as those type of thoughts creep in now, I just throw them out of my mind straight away. If I was a lion, I would just bite their heads off – I would just eat them and spit out the bones!

So whenever those thoughts come in, just say "no" and write your goals down again. Yes, you've done it before. But writing a big goal down again ignites the fire. I know that if I write, *"I have 1000 properties which produce £600,000 a month net profit, which puts me in nearly one percent of high-net individuals in the world. I start to mix in these circles, which benefits me and my family. I become well-known worldwide,"* that instantly puts me in a different mindset to that of a hyena or a sloth.

It makes me sit up a bit straighter in my car or at my desk. It really does work when you write it down and especially if you then say it out loud. It reminds you of your reason why. When you're lacking motivation and you can't be bothered, it's the best thing to do.

Distractions are always going to be there, but you don't have to entertain them. It's your choice how long you stay with a distraction. You can cut them out of your life if you really want to. You just have to design your life in a way where there is no time for distractions. If you lose a lot of money, you can make it back. But if you lose a lot of time with distractions or working for earned income, you won't ever get that back.

PASSIVE INCOME VS EARNED INCOME

The life of your wildest dreams probably isn't about working 50 hours a week. You probably want to be doing something else with your time. So, the only way really to achieve that is to have passive income. This then gives you more time to do things that you want to do for yourself and for your family.

So, passive income is more important than earned income. A golden rule is to aim to spend more time making passive income than earned income. Gear yourself up to investing every bit of money that you can into something that produces passive income.

Yes, you have to get earned income in the first place to then invest it in passive income. But slowly, with time, you need to put in more energy and commit more time to getting passive income than earned income.

With earned income, you have to work for it. With passive income, you get paid whether you're on holiday, in bed, at the gym, whether in hospital or at work. You get paid no matter what. This is the crucial difference that makes all the difference!

A lion approaches every situation with energy, passion, and everything he's got.

I've aimed in this book to teach you how to have a lion's mindset in every single part of your life so that you don't put any restrictions or limitations on yourself. This mindset allows you to approach every situation with energy, with passion, with everything you've got. A lion might choose to sit under a tree. Or he might want to go and eat gazelles and zebras. He might want to extend its territory or challenge another older lion and take over his pride. They do what they want, because they don't hold themselves back.

MONEY MINDSET

Everyone's got an idea of how much money they think they can earn and how much they think they're worth. A good analogy is a container. For example, if you think you are worth £100,000 a year, your container can only fit £100,000 in it.

If you start to make £150,000, it feels like this is £50,000 is over and above what your container should be holding. So you'll start to recklessly blow it and spend willy-nilly on stupid things – because it's not in alignment with what you believe you should be receiving. (That's why people win the Lottery and then go skint after they win £1 million as they recklessly spend the rest).

Trying to increase the size of this container will always keep you on the right path. The way to increase the capacity of your container is to surround yourself with people who are earning more than you, and who set bigger goals than you, because that forces you to think differently.

MIND TRICKS

Set yourself big goals. The second you go from having a goal of making £1 million to having a bigger goal, say of £10 million, you are instantly you forced to think differently. Because your habits, behaviours, choices, action plan, business plan are so much bigger at £10 million. Just by setting that goal higher, you are forced to act differently and do different things. You might achieve £7 million or £8 million, but it's always going to be more than if you set a goal of just £1 million.

A lion will still hunt an antelope even if it has dangerous-looking horns.

If you're going to set a goal, you might as well make it a big one. If a large antelope with dangerous-looking horns walks past a lion, he isn't going to just say, "Oh, go on, injured antelope, you keep walking. You're taller than me and your horns look a bit too sharp." No, he's not. He might have already eaten, but he still has cubs who might be hungry. Even if the antelope is taller than him and has horns that might pierce him, he's still going to go for it.

There are no limits – only the limits you put on yourself.

Sometimes you'll want to go after an elephant. Sometimes you'll need 10 other lions around you to chase down your goal, to capture your prize. So sometimes you need to have other good lions around you.

There are no limits – only the limits you put on yourself.

BE A LION: 90-DAY JOURNAL

If you've enjoyed this book and would like to commit to developing a lion's mindset, you can also buy my "Be A Lion: 90-Day Journal" that accompanies my book on Amazon.

CONNECT WITH ME

Take pictures of your journey as a lion – include photos of yourself; sections of this book that you find helpful; quotes that you like; your list of goals, etc. Then, post it and tag me on Instagram.

Printed in Great Britain
by Amazon

76669244R00142